Guided by Light: The Story of the Ismailis - Faith, Resilience, and Global Impact

Guided by Light: The Story of the Ismailis - Faith, Resilience, and Global Impact

Guided by Light: The Story of the Ismailis - Faith, Resilience, and Global Impact

Francis Williams

"Diversity is not a reason to put up walls,
but rather to open windows.
It is not a burden,
it is a blessing."

Aga Khan Development Network

"Where there is love and wisdom,
there is no fear and no division."

St. Francis of Assisi

For Zahra and Eilidh,

May Love, Peace and Joy

Accompany You Always

September 5th 2025

Copyright Page

Guided by Light: The Story of the Ismailis — Faith, Resilience, and Global Impact
© 2025 Francis Williams
All rights reserved.

No part of this publication may be reproduced, stored in a retrieval system, or transmitted in any form or by any means — electronic, mechanical, photocopying, recording, or otherwise — without the prior written permission of the copyright holder, except in the case of brief quotations embodied in critical articles or reviews.

This is a work of nonfiction. While every effort has been made to ensure accuracy, the author does not assume responsibility for any errors or omissions. This book is not affiliated with or officially endorsed by the Ismaili Imamat, the Aga Khan Development Network, or the institutions referenced herein.

Cover design, layout, and formatting by the Author
Research assistance and content support provided by AI tools developed by OpenAI.

ISBN: 978-1-997668-41-1
First Edition, 2025

Printed in USA

"Guided by Light: The Story of the Ismailis — Faith, Resilience, and Global Impact"

Table of Contents

Introduction 1

Chapter 1: The Seeds of Faith — Birth of the Ismaili Tradition 3

Chapter 2: A Hidden Flame — The Period of Concealment 7

Chapter 3: The Golden Age — The Fatimid Caliphate 11

Chapter 4: Towers of Resistance — Alamut and the "Assassins" 15

Chapter 5: Scattered, Yet Strong — Survival after Alamut 19

Chapter 6: The Aga Khan Legacy — A Modern Imamate 23

Chapter 7: The Heart of Belief — God, Prophets, and the Living Imam 27

Chapter 8: Unveiling Inner Truths — Esoteric Wisdom and *Ta'wil* ... 31

Chapter 9: Mind and Spirit — The Embrace of Reason 35

Chapter 10: Rituals Reimagined — Practices and Pillars 39

Chapter 11: A Global Tapestry — The Modern Ismaili Diaspora 43

Chapter 12: Service Beyond Borders — The Aga Khan Development Network 47

Chapter 13: The Spirit of Pluralism — Dialogue and Volunteerism ... 51

Chapter 14: Beauty and Legacy — Art, Architecture, and Culture 55

Chapter 15: An Enduring Journey — Lessons for the Future 59

Timeline of Major Events in Ismaili History 63

Bibliography 67

Glossary 69

Disclaimer

This book is intended as an informative and narrative exploration of Ismaili history, beliefs, and community life, designed for general audiences. While every effort has been made to ensure accuracy and clarity, this work does not claim to represent official Ismaili doctrinal positions or serve as an authoritative religious text. Readers are encouraged to consult primary sources and official community publications for deeper theological study or scholarly research.

The stories, interpretations, and perspectives presented here are drawn from a wide range of historical, academic, and publicly available resources, and aim to provide a friendly, accessible introduction to the subject matter. Any errors or omissions are the responsibility of the author.

Acknowledgements

This book was made possible thanks to the collective contributions of scholars, historians, community members, and countless individuals who have dedicated their lives to studying and preserving the Ismaili tradition.

Special appreciation is extended to the authors and researchers whose works are cited throughout this book and to the institutions and organizations, including The Institute of Ismaili Studies and the Aga Khan Development Network, whose publications and resources were invaluable.

Additionally, this book was conceptualized, drafted, and refined with the support of advanced AI tools for research assistance, content development, editing, and structural organization. These tools played an important role in helping bring together complex historical narratives and spiritual concepts into a cohesive and engaging reader-friendly format.

To all those who keep the light of learning, service, and pluralism alive in their communities — thank you.

Introduction

In a world woven from countless threads of belief, the story of the Ismailis gleams like a shimmering tapestry of faith, resilience, and hope. Imagine standing on a mountain ridge at dawn, the light just beginning to brush the peaks with gold. This light, subtle yet powerful, is much like the guiding spirit of the Ismaili community — enduring, adaptive, and always reaching for the horizon.

The Ismaili Muslims, a branch of Shia Islam, trace their story to the 8th century CE, arising from a profound question that has shaped much of Islamic history: Who should lead the faithful after the Prophet Muhammad? The Shi'a tradition, in general, upheld that leadership should pass through the Prophet's family, but within this view emerged the Ismailis, who followed the line of Imam Isma'il, the eldest son of Imam Ja'far al-Sadiq. This choice was more than a family matter — it signaled a vision of spiritual continuity anchored in a living, present guide, known as the Imam.

From this early decision, a remarkable journey unfolded. For centuries, Ismailis navigated the shadows, concealing their faith to survive in an often hostile world. This era of taqiyya — the practice of pious dissimulation — was not just a strategy of survival but a testament to an unyielding commitment to their inner truth. In the hidden corners of cities and the quiet valleys of mountains, their spiritual flame continued to burn, unseen but never extinguished.

Emerging from secrecy, the Ismailis stepped into the light of the Fatimid Caliphate in North Africa and Egypt, establishing an empire where intellect and faith walked hand in hand. Cairo bloomed into a beacon of learning and culture, housing scholars, poets, physicians, and architects. Under Fatimid rule, the community demonstrated that faith need not oppose reason but could illuminate it, fostering a society where diverse ideas flourished like gardens in spring.

Yet, the story did not rest on imperial grandeur. The community faced fragmentation, internal strife, and external enemies. The "Assassins" of Alamut, often misunderstood as fanatics, were in fact a people using strategy over brute force to preserve their freedom against overwhelming odds. Even when Alamut fell to the Mongols, and many believed the Ismailis had vanished into history's mists, the community merely transformed, blending into local societies while guarding their spiritual essence.

In the modern era, the leadership of the Aga Khans has guided the community into a new chapter — one defined not by political rule but by a global mission of compassion and service. The Aga Khan Development Network (AKDN) reaches millions, building hospitals, schools, and bridges (both literal and metaphorical) across continents. The community's ethic of volunteerism and pluralism shines brightly, reminding us that faith, at its best, is a force for unity rather than division.

Today, Ismailis are scattered across more than 35 countries, from the snowy valleys of Tajikistan to the bustling streets of Toronto, from the deserts of Syria to the plains of East Africa. They are engineers, artists, farmers, and entrepreneurs — bound together by a belief in a living Imam who embodies the continuity of divine guidance.

"Guided by Light" invites you to journey into this story: a chronicle of hidden sages and philosopher-kings, of resilience woven into every heart, and of a timeless search for balance between the spiritual and the material. It is a tale that speaks not just to one community, but to all who seek to understand how faith can evolve, endure, and illuminate the shared human path.

Chapter 1: The Seeds of Faith — Birth of the Ismaili Tradition

To truly understand the journey of the Ismailis, we must begin in the fertile soil of early Islamic history, where the seeds of their faith were sown amidst love, loyalty, and disputes over divine leadership. Picture the desert winds swirling around Medina, carrying whispers of a new message that had just begun to transform the Arabian Peninsula and, eventually, the entire world.

After the passing of the Prophet Muhammad in 632 CE, his followers faced a profound question: Who would guide them spiritually and politically? While most Muslims, who would later be called Sunnis, chose to follow elected caliphs, a group of devoted believers insisted that leadership belonged to the Prophet's family — the Ahl al-Bayt — specifically to Ali ibn Abi Talib, the Prophet's cousin and son-in-law. This group became known as the Shi'a, meaning "party" or "followers" of Ali.

Ali's life was marked by deep spiritual devotion and a reputation for unmatched wisdom and justice. His followers believed that he was more than just a capable leader — they saw in him the divinely designated inheritor of the Prophet's spiritual authority. After Ali's martyrdom in 661 CE, the mantle of leadership, known as the Imamate, continued through his descendants, each believed to be a guiding light in turbulent times.

This line of spiritual leaders progressed to Imam Ja'far al-Sadiq, the sixth Imam, renowned for his vast knowledge in both religious and scientific fields. He attracted scholars from all corners of the Islamic world, and his debates on theology, philosophy, and natural sciences became legendary. But it was after his death in 765 CE that the path of Shi'ism would branch in ways that forever shaped Islamic history.

Here begins the story of the Ismailis. Imam Ja'far al-Sadiq had named his eldest son, Isma'il, as his successor — a designation known as *nass*, a divinely inspired appointment meant to be beyond dispute. However, Isma'il passed away before his father, creating a crisis. Many of Ja'far's followers accepted his younger son, Musa al-Kadhim, as the next Imam. They would later become known as the Twelvers, the largest group within Shi'a Islam today.

Yet, a devoted segment held firmly to the belief that Isma'il was the rightful Imam, or that the Imamate should continue through his progeny. They maintained that Isma'il's designation could not be nullified by death and that the divine light of guidance — known as *nur* — continued through his son, Muhammad ibn Isma'il. These believers would come to be called the Ismailis, taking their name from this defining moment of devotion and loyalty.

Choosing this path was not a mere theological preference; it was a profound act of faith and trust in the continuity of divine guidance. For the Ismailis, the Imam was not just a learned scholar or a political figure — he was the living, present proof (*hujjat*) of God's will on earth. The Imam carried the inner meaning of the Quran (*batin*) and was the bridge between the visible world and the divine.

While this belief set them apart, it also set them on a path of vulnerability. In those early centuries, the Islamic empire was vast and often intolerant of diverging interpretations of faith. The Abbasid caliphs, ruling from Baghdad, were especially wary of any movements that might challenge their authority. In this atmosphere, Ismailis found themselves frequently accused of sedition and faced waves of persecution. It was in these crucibles of hardship that their traditions of resilience and adaptability were forged.

One cannot help but imagine those early Ismaili followers, gathering in hushed meetings under the cover of night, passing secret messages, and studying the esoteric meanings of scripture with trembling yet determined hands. They clung to the vision of a community guided by a living Imam, a beacon of light in an otherwise dark and often hostile world.

During these formative years, the Ismailis began to develop a sophisticated network of missionaries, known as *da'i*, who spread the teachings of the Imamate across vast territories, from North Africa to Persia and beyond. These missionaries were not mere proselytizers; they were deeply learned, capable of engaging in complex theological debates and offering intellectual and spiritual support to new believers.

Their teachings emphasized that religion was not simply a matter of rigid rituals and literal interpretations. Instead, the Ismailis taught that faith was a dynamic journey inward, seeking the deeper, hidden truths beneath the surface of words and practices. This idea, known as *ta'wil* — the esoteric interpretation — became a hallmark of Ismaili spirituality. It allowed them to adapt, to remain flexible, and to find meaning even in the most adverse conditions.

Their emphasis on inner meaning and spiritual wisdom attracted many thinkers and seekers who felt suffocated by rigid orthodoxy. Through quiet perseverance and subtlety, the Ismaili movement spread and took root, like seeds carried by the wind, finding unexpected gardens in remote mountain valleys and bustling urban centers alike.

These early Ismailis also developed the concept of *taqiyya*, or pious dissimulation, as a means of protecting themselves while remaining true to their inner beliefs. This practice allowed them to outwardly conform to dominant religious norms when under threat, while maintaining their unique faith in private. Though some may view this with suspicion, for the Ismailis, it was a necessary measure of survival and a demonstration of spiritual steadfastness rather than weakness.

Their clandestine networks and ability to endure oppression with dignity laid the foundation for what would later blossom into powerful and visible manifestations of Ismaili identity. The Fatimid Caliphate, the Alamut strongholds, and the modern global community all trace their roots back to these first seeds of belief, carefully nurtured and fiercely protected.

The story of the Ismailis' birth is thus not merely about theological schism but about the courage to stand by a vision, even when it means walking alone. It is about a community that chose the difficult road of hidden gatherings and whispered prayers rather than abandoning their conviction in a living, guiding Imam. It is a story of hope, of hidden strength, and of a light that refuses to be extinguished.

As we move forward in this book, we will see how this foundational faith transformed over centuries, blooming into golden ages and surviving through the darkest storms. But it all began here — with a choice that would define a people, a choice to believe that divine guidance did not belong only to history but continued, alive, and pulsing in the present through the Imam.

And so, from a desert dispute over succession to hidden meetings under starlit skies, the Ismaili story begins: a testament to faith, courage, and the unyielding human desire to seek the light beyond the veil.

Chapter 2: A Hidden Flame — The Period of Concealment

As the early Ismaili community began to grow, their unwavering devotion to a living Imam set them apart, attracting curiosity, admiration, and, unfortunately, suspicion and hostility. The powerful Abbasid caliphate, with its sprawling bureaucratic machinery and immense military might, viewed any alternative religious authority as a direct threat to its legitimacy. For the Ismailis, this meant that the simple act of practicing their faith openly could be a death sentence.

So, how does a community survive when the world seems to close in from every side? The Ismailis found their answer in an extraordinary strategy of resilience: they turned inward and learned to live like a hidden flame, burning bright but unseen.

This period is known in their history as the *dawr al-satr*, or the "period of concealment." Spanning approximately 150 years, it is one of the most fascinating chapters of their story — a time when the identity of the Imam was hidden to protect him and his followers. It was not merely about survival but about preserving a profound spiritual lineage, a sacred trust that had to be safeguarded at all costs.

Imagine a small village at the foot of the Syrian mountains in the 9th century. Under the soft glow of oil lamps, a group gathers in a dimly lit room. The doors are bolted shut, and the windows covered with thick fabric. Inside, an elder speaks in a hushed yet fervent tone, revealing the deeper, esoteric meanings of scripture. No one dares to write these words down; they live in the hearts and minds of the listeners alone. The atmosphere is tense but electric — here, faith is not a matter of routine but an act of courage and a declaration of identity.

During this era, the Ismaili community established a highly organized underground missionary network known as the *da'wa*, meaning "summons" or "invitation." At its head was the *hujja* — the "proof" — an authoritative figure who acted as the intermediary between the hidden

Imam and the community. The *da'wa* was an intricate web of spiritual teachers, community organizers, and traveling preachers who carried the message far and wide, all under the cloak of secrecy.

These da'is, or missionaries, often traveled disguised as traders or scholars. They visited marketplaces and caravanserais, striking up casual conversations that, with subtlety and patience, would turn toward matters of faith and deeper truths. Their method was never about loud proclamations but rather about gentle persuasion and personal connection. The *da'wa* became both a lifeline and a lifeblood, keeping the spiritual heart of the community beating during the years of danger and darkness.

The strategy of *taqiyya*, or pious dissimulation, played a central role during this time. Rather than outright confrontation, Ismailis learned to wear a cloak of outward conformity. They would pray alongside Sunnis in mosques, celebrate the same festivals, and recite familiar public creeds, all while nurturing their unique understanding of faith in secret gatherings. In many ways, this was a sophisticated form of spiritual camouflage, allowing the community to blend in while remaining true to its core.

This outward conformity should not be mistaken for compromise or weakness. In fact, it was a powerful testament to the community's adaptability and ingenuity. The practice of *taqiyya* was seen as a shield, a necessary defense in a world where revealing one's true beliefs could lead to execution or worse. It was an act of spiritual preservation, a silent promise whispered from generation to generation: "We will endure. We will carry the flame."

Underneath this veil of secrecy, the Ismailis were developing a rich intellectual and spiritual tradition. The hidden Imams, though physically absent from public view, continued to guide their followers through the *hujja* and *da'wa* networks. Philosophical and theological debates flourished in clandestine study circles, and scholars crafted intricate interpretations of the Quran, emphasizing its inner, esoteric meanings (*batin*).

This focus on esoteric knowledge became a defining feature of Ismaili thought. Unlike purely literal readings of scripture, the Ismailis believed that true understanding required peeling away layers of meaning to reach the spiritual essence. They saw the Imam as the key to unlocking these deeper truths, a living guide who could lead them beyond the outward forms to the divine light within.

The hidden flame of Ismaili faith did not just flicker quietly in the Middle East. Through the *da'wa*, Ismaili ideas spread east to Persia and Central Asia and west to North Africa. In places as distant as Yemen and Sindh (in present-day Pakistan), communities began to sprout, connected by invisible threads of devotion and shared understanding.

These far-flung communities often developed strong local identities, woven from both Ismaili teachings and regional cultures. This diversity would later become one of the great strengths of the Ismaili world — a network of believers linked not by a single language or homeland but by a shared spiritual vision.

The hidden era also sowed the seeds for one of the most significant political and spiritual revolutions in Islamic history: the establishment of the Fatimid Caliphate. In the 9th century, in the Syrian town of Salamiyya, the hidden Imams coordinated a daring plan to establish an Ismaili state. From their concealed headquarters, emissaries spread into North Africa, preparing the ground among local tribes and populations disenchanted with Abbasid rule.

The vision was audacious. Imagine small, secretive meetings turning into a groundswell of support that would one day rise to challenge one of the most powerful empires of its time. It was a testament to the power of ideas — and to the courage of those willing to carry them forward at immense personal risk.

Throughout the *dawr al-satr*, countless individuals gave their lives to protect the community and keep the faith alive. Their stories often went unrecorded, their names lost to history. Yet, their sacrifices became the foundation upon which later triumphs were built. Their quiet heroism echoes through the ages, a reminder that sometimes the most profound acts of faith are not those shouted from rooftops but those whispered in the dark, when no one else is watching.

By the time the Fatimid Caliphate would emerge in North Africa in the early 10th century, the Ismaili community had been forged in the fires of persecution and secrecy. Their sense of identity was not fragile but tempered and strong, shaped by a theology that emphasized both outer discipline and inner enlightenment.

As we close this chapter, we can almost hear the echoes of those secret gatherings — the soft recitations of esoteric verses, the careful guidance of a *da'i*, the shared, silent understanding that they were part of something greater than themselves. The hidden flame, though invisible to the world, was alive and growing stronger.

This period of concealment was not simply about hiding; it was about transformation. The Ismailis learned to turn adversity into spiritual fortitude, persecution into inner clarity, and fear into a quiet, unwavering courage. They emerged from these hidden years not diminished but emboldened, ready to step onto the grand stage of history and reveal to the world the brilliance of their faith.

In the next chapter, we will see how this hidden flame erupted into a dazzling light during the Fatimid Caliphate — an era where the Ismailis not only survived but thrived, building an empire that would become a beacon of learning, culture, and pluralism for centuries to come.

Chapter 3: The Golden Age — The Fatimid Caliphate

After decades of hiding in shadows, whispering prayers in secret rooms, and spreading teachings through covert networks, the Ismailis finally stepped into the sunlight of history. This emergence was not a timid appearance but a bold, radiant dawn — the rise of the Fatimid Caliphate.

Picture North Africa in the early 10th century. A landscape of shifting sands, distant mountains, and bustling coastal cities alive with traders from across the Mediterranean and beyond. Here, in 909 CE, an event unfolded that would forever change Islamic history: the establishment of the Fatimid Caliphate. At its heart stood an Ismaili Imam who was no longer hidden but declared himself openly as both a spiritual and political leader.

The seeds of this transformation were sown in Salamiyya, a modest Syrian town where the hidden Imams had taken refuge. From this clandestine base, emissaries ventured forth, weaving alliances and planting the dream of a just, spiritually guided state. Among the most influential of these missions was the work among the Kutama Berbers of North Africa. Disillusioned with the distant and often oppressive Abbasid rulers, the Berbers found hope and purpose in the Ismaili message.

In 909 CE, their support culminated in victory. ʿAbd Allāh al-Mahdī, a descendant of Prophet Muhammad through Fatima and Ali, was proclaimed the first Fatimid Caliph in Ifriqiya (modern-day Tunisia and eastern Algeria). He took on the title "al-Mahdī," signaling the arrival of a divinely guided leader who would usher in a new age of justice and enlightenment. For the Ismailis, this was a moment of vindication and profound joy — the hidden Imam had become visible to the world, and their long-suppressed faith could finally flourish in the open.

Under the Fatimids, the Ismailis built a state that was as remarkable for its intellectual vibrancy as for its military and political power. The Caliphate expanded rapidly, and by 969 CE, the Fatimids captured Egypt and established Cairo as their new capital. Imagine arriving in Cairo during its golden age: a city of grand mosques, splendid gardens, shimmering minarets, and bustling markets. It wasn't just a capital; it was a living testament to the Fatimid vision of a society where faith and reason walked hand in hand.

Central to this vision was the creation of institutions that nurtured knowledge and encouraged free inquiry. The Al-Azhar Mosque, founded in 970 CE, soon transformed into a university — one of the oldest in the world — where scholars from across the Islamic world gathered. Here, philosophy, theology, law, and the natural sciences were taught side by side. Students debated the works of Aristotle and Plato, discussed the mysteries of the cosmos, and explored the depths of the Quran's esoteric meanings. It was a place where questions were not feared but celebrated.

Alongside Al-Azhar stood the Dar al-'Ilm, or House of Knowledge, a monumental library and learning center housing hundreds of thousands of manuscripts. Think of it as the internet of its time — a repository of human thought and achievement. Scholars, poets, astronomers, and physicians roamed its halls, exchanging ideas in an atmosphere of curiosity and mutual respect. The Fatimid leaders believed that the quest for knowledge was a form of worship, a way to understand the divine creation more deeply.

This intellectual openness extended to everyday life. The arts flourished in Fatimid Cairo, from exquisite pottery and shimmering glasswork to textiles woven with intricate patterns and symbols. The Fatimid artisans developed rock crystal ewers so finely carved that they seemed almost ethereal, shimmering like moonlight in a desert oasis. Architectural innovations turned the city into a canvas of geometric harmony and spiritual symbolism.

Economically, the Fatimids transformed Egypt into a global hub of trade. Positioned at the crossroads of Africa, Asia, and Europe, Cairo became a bustling marketplace where merchants from Venice, India, Sub-Saharan Africa, and beyond converged. Spices, silks, precious stones, and scientific instruments changed hands, along with stories and ideas. The Fatimid navy dominated the Mediterranean, and Egypt became the engine powering an interconnected world economy. This prosperity not only filled the state's coffers but also funded public welfare projects, hospitals, and schools, improving the quality of life for countless people.

The spiritual leadership of the Fatimid Imams was integral to this societal flourishing. Unlike rulers who separated religious and worldly matters, the Fatimid Caliphs embodied both spiritual and temporal authority. They saw governance as a sacred trust, an extension of their role as Imams. This holistic vision meant that religious teachings guided policy, but not in a rigid or dogmatic way. Instead, it fostered a culture of tolerance and inclusiveness. Christians, Jews, and various Muslim sects found space to practice and contribute to the fabric of Fatimid society.

Yet, even in this golden age, shadows loomed. Internal disputes over succession began to crack the unity of the Caliphate. In 1094 CE, after the death of Imam Mustansir bi'llah, a major schism split the Ismaili world into two main branches: the Nizaris, who supported his elder son Nizar, and the Musta'lis, who accepted the younger son Musta'li. This division deeply weakened the state, undermining the centralized control that had held it together.

Despite these internal fractures, the Fatimid Caliphate endured for nearly two centuries, a remarkable testament to its resilience and the strength of its institutions. But as the 12th century progressed, external pressures mounted. Crusaders encroached from the west, while internal revolts and military mutinies sapped the state's vitality. Eventually, in 1171 CE, Saladin, appointed as vizier, formally ended Fatimid rule, reinstating Sunni authority in Egypt and confining the Fatimid family under house arrest.

The fall of the Fatimid Caliphate was a moment of profound loss for the Ismaili community. Their empire, a beacon of learning and cultural brilliance, had collapsed. Yet, even in defeat, they carried forward the intellectual and spiritual legacies cultivated during those luminous centuries in Cairo.

The Fatimid era offers us a vivid lesson: even under the most splendid domes and in the most opulent palaces, human institutions are vulnerable to the same flaws that affect all communities — ambition, rivalry, and the unpredictable winds of history. But while the political structure crumbled, the underlying spirit of the Ismaili faith endured, carried forward by individuals and families who refused to let the light go out.

Today, as we walk through Cairo's historic streets, visit Al-Azhar, or admire the delicate Fatimid art in museums around the world, we are reminded of that golden chapter when faith and reason coexisted in a delicate dance. The Fatimid Caliphate stands not merely as a political memory but as a living inspiration, urging us to seek knowledge, celebrate diversity, and hold fast to our spiritual values even as we navigate the complex realities of the world.

As we close this chapter and look ahead, we will see how, after the fall of their empire, the Ismailis once again found themselves on the edge of survival. They would retreat into the mountains, creating strongholds that seemed like legends out of a distant epic — Alamut and the rise of the so-called "Assassins." But as we will discover, this new phase was not merely about warfare and defense but also about preserving the essence of their faith, pushing the boundaries of philosophy, and preparing for future renewal.

The story of the Fatimid Caliphate is, at its heart, a love letter to the union of faith and intellect, a testament to what is possible when a community dares to imagine a world illuminated by knowledge and guided by a higher purpose.

Chapter 4: Towers of Resistance — Alamut and the "Assassins"

When the Fatimid Caliphate fell in 1171 CE, it was as though a great lantern had been extinguished in the Muslim world. The once-vibrant city of Cairo, with its bustling markets, luminous scholars, and peaceful gardens, slowly transformed under new rulers. But while the physical empire crumbled, the spirit of the Ismaili faith refused to be buried beneath the sands of history. Instead, it took on a new and unexpected shape — high in the mountains of northern Iran, in a castle that would become the stuff of legend: Alamut.

Imagine the rugged Alborz mountain range, where snow-capped peaks stand watch over deep valleys and dense forests. Tucked into this wild, seemingly inaccessible terrain stood Alamut Castle, perched dramatically atop a narrow rock formation. It was here, in 1090 CE — even before the Fatimid decline was complete — that a brilliant and fiercely determined figure, Hasan-i Sabbah, laid the foundation of a new Ismaili stronghold.

Hasan-i Sabbah was no ordinary leader. A scholar, strategist, and devout believer, he envisioned Alamut not merely as a military fortress but as a sanctuary of learning and spiritual training. Under his guidance, Alamut became the heart of what is now known as the Nizari Ismaili state, a network of fortresses scattered across Persia and Syria. Each fortress operated like a miniature world, self-sufficient and strategically positioned to resist much larger forces.

From the perspective of powerful neighbors — the Seljuks, Crusaders, and other Sunni rulers — the Nizari Ismailis quickly gained a reputation for being both elusive and formidable. They became known in the Western world as the "Assassins," a name shrouded in myth and misunderstanding. The term likely emerged from the Arabic *hashashin*, referring either to their alleged use of hashish (a claim most historians now dismiss) or as a derogatory term used by their enemies to paint them as drugged fanatics.

In reality, the Nizaris' use of targeted assassinations was a carefully calculated form of asymmetric warfare. Faced with overwhelming enemies and lacking large armies, the community developed a strategy to eliminate key figures who threatened their survival. Instead of waging full-scale wars that would likely annihilate them, they sent small, highly trained groups called *fidā'īs* — "devotees" willing to sacrifice their lives if necessary — to strike against political and military leaders.

These acts were not random or driven by bloodlust. Rather, they were precise, surgical strikes intended to deter aggression and protect the community. In many ways, it was a brutal but necessary expression of self-defense, a desperate measure to keep alive a faith that had been persecuted for centuries.

Beyond this image of shadowy figures and midnight blades, Alamut was a place of vibrant intellectual life. Under Hasan-i Sabbah and his successors, it housed impressive libraries, laboratories, and gardens. Imagine scholars in flowing robes debating philosophy, astronomy, and mathematics under the moonlit sky, with the silhouette of the fortress walls standing guard around them. Here, the esoteric teachings of the Ismaili tradition — the deep, inner meanings of the Quran and the universe — continued to flourish.

This intellectual environment produced works that would later influence Islamic thought far beyond the Nizari community. The emphasis on *ta'wil*, or esoteric interpretation, reached new heights. Scholars explored the relationship between the visible world (*zahir*) and the hidden spiritual reality (*batin*), delving into the mysteries of creation, human existence, and divine purpose.

Life in Alamut and the other Nizari fortresses demanded extraordinary resilience. Supplies had to be meticulously managed; every piece of food, every arrowhead, every candle mattered. The inhabitants lived under the constant threat of siege, knowing that at any moment, their fortress could become an island in a sea of hostile forces. Yet, within those high walls, there existed a sense of freedom and spiritual clarity that many found worth every risk.

While the myth of the "Assassins" spread through Europe and entered popular imagination (even inspiring centuries-later stories, novels, and video games), the real story was more profound. The Nizaris were a small, determined community using intelligence, strategy, and devotion to protect their identity and values. They became legendary not because they sought power for its own sake, but because they sought to preserve the light of their faith against the overwhelming darkness of persecution.

The golden age of Alamut eventually came to a tragic and violent end. In 1256 CE, the Mongol Empire, expanding under Hulagu Khan, set its sights on the mountain fortresses of the Nizaris. The Mongols, known for their brutal efficiency, surrounded Alamut and systematically dismantled its defenses. Imam Rukn al-Din Khurshah, the last ruler of Alamut, was forced to surrender, and the fortress fell. The libraries, with their precious manuscripts, were set aflame, their knowledge turned to ash that drifted down the valleys like ghostly snow.

The fall of Alamut marked a devastating blow. Many believed the Ismailis were utterly destroyed, their story ending amidst smoldering ruins. Yet, this was far from the truth. Like a river finding new channels after a dam collapse, the community flowed into new regions and forms. Small groups of Nizaris survived by blending into local populations, practicing *taqiyya* once again to avoid detection. In places like Persia, Syria, and Central Asia, they quietly maintained their traditions, passing down teachings in whispered lessons behind closed doors.

Among the most significant new centers of survival was the mountainous region of Badakhshan (today part of Tajikistan and northeastern Afghanistan). Here, the seeds of Ismaili faith found new soil. In this remote and rugged terrain, protected by isolation and the strength of mountain people, the community endured and even thrived over the centuries.

The Alamut period was a crucible — a time when the Ismailis demonstrated that survival is not merely about having walls and weapons but about the strength of spirit and unity of purpose. While they became known to the world as "Assassins," their true legacy lies in their unyielding commitment to intellectual exploration, spiritual depth, and communal resilience.

Today, Alamut stands in ruins, its stones silent witnesses to a turbulent past. Yet for the Ismailis, it remains a powerful symbol — a testament to the courage of a community that refused to disappear, a monument to the balance between defense and knowledge, between sword and pen, between survival and the eternal search for meaning.

As we look beyond Alamut, we find a community reshaped once again, emerging from hidden valleys and scattered villages into the modern world. In the chapters to come, we will see how they navigated new threats, found new leaders, and ultimately transformed into a global community known not for assassinations but for humanitarianism, education, and service to all humankind.

Chapter 5: Scattered, Yet Strong — Survival after Alamut

The fall of Alamut in 1256 CE could have been the final chapter in the story of the Ismailis. The Mongol onslaught was so devastating, so total, that it appeared to many outsiders as though the community had been erased from the pages of history. The once-mighty fortresses were reduced to rubble, their libraries burned, their leaders captured or executed. Observers might have thought that the flame of Ismaili faith had finally been snuffed out.

But the Ismailis, true to their spirit, were not so easily extinguished. Even as the embers of Alamut cooled, the community was already finding ways to survive, adapt, and preserve its light. Like seeds scattered by a strong wind, Ismailis took root in distant and unexpected places, carrying their faith in their hearts rather than in stone walls.

In the immediate aftermath of Alamut's destruction, many Ismailis retreated into the remote mountains of Persia, Syria, and Central Asia. Here, the rough terrain provided a natural shield against prying eyes and marauding armies. In these isolated regions, they practiced *taqiyya* — the art of dissimulation — with renewed intensity. Outwardly, they appeared as ordinary Sunni Muslims or Sufis, blending seamlessly into their surroundings. Inwardly, they continued to pass down their spiritual teachings, often from parent to child, as a treasured family secret.

One of the most remarkable examples of this resilience took shape in the region of Badakhshan. Nestled between towering peaks and deep valleys, Badakhshan straddles parts of modern-day Tajikistan and northeastern Afghanistan. This landscape, breathtaking in its beauty yet harsh and unforgiving, became a sanctuary for the Ismailis. Here, under the cover of snow-capped mountains and rugged passes, they preserved their traditions largely undisturbed for centuries.

A key figure in the establishment of Ismailism in Badakhshan was Nasir-i Khusraw, an 11th-century Persian poet, philosopher, and missionary.

After a profound spiritual awakening, Nasir-i Khusraw embarked on a seven-year journey through the Islamic world, eventually arriving at the Fatimid court in Cairo. Deeply inspired, he returned to Persia and dedicated his life to spreading Ismaili teachings. His eloquent writings, blending poetry with profound spiritual insights, became cherished texts for the community in Badakhshan and beyond. Even today, his poetry remains a source of guidance and inspiration for Ismailis, offering a bridge between faith and daily life.

Outside of Central Asia, Ismailis also found refuge in parts of Syria, particularly in the mountainous areas of Masyaf, and in small pockets throughout Iran and India. In each new homeland, they adapted to local customs while quietly nurturing their distinctive beliefs. Some joined Sufi orders or adopted the language and dress of their Sunni neighbors. These acts were not betrayals of faith but ingenious strategies for survival — a way to remain true to the essence of their teachings while avoiding deadly persecution.

The centuries following Alamut were not easy. Ismailis faced recurrent waves of hostility and suspicion. They were often blamed for rebellions or conspiracies, accused of being mysterious or untrustworthy due to their secretive ways. Yet, despite the risks, they managed to preserve an unbroken line of Imams. This continuity was not always visible to the outside world, but for the faithful, it was a source of hope and a sign that divine guidance remained alive.

The spiritual leadership during these difficult centuries was crucial. The Imams continued to guide their followers, sometimes from deep seclusion, maintaining contact through trusted representatives and coded messages. This hidden line of communication created a sense of intimacy and connection, reinforcing the idea that, even in the darkest times, the Imam was present — a living embodiment of divine wisdom.

Gradually, as centuries passed, the Ismailis began to reemerge more visibly in certain regions. In the Indian subcontinent, particularly in the areas of Gujarat and Sindh, Ismaili communities started to thrive. Trade and commerce offered opportunities to build economic strength and foster communal networks. Over time, some Indian Ismailis developed into the

Khoja community, known for their entrepreneurial spirit and strong communal bonds. While they maintained their religious identity, they also contributed actively to the broader social and economic life of their regions.

In Persia, small Ismaili settlements persisted, often in rugged mountain villages that seemed cut off from the rest of the world. The villagers lived simple lives, farming the land and herding animals, but their homes were filled with whispered stories of past glories and teachings handed down through the generations.

As they rebuilt, the Ismailis never abandoned their commitment to knowledge and intellectual inquiry. Even in remote areas, they preserved and studied texts on philosophy, science, and spiritual interpretation. The emphasis on *ta'wil*, the esoteric interpretation of scripture, continued to shape their worldview, allowing them to adapt to changing circumstances without losing the essence of their faith.

The constant practice of *taqiyya* not only ensured physical survival but also deepened the community's sense of inner identity. Living a double life demanded a heightened awareness of the difference between outward appearance and inner truth — a concept at the heart of Ismaili theology. It reminded them daily that the visible world (*zahir*) is merely a veil over deeper spiritual realities (*batin*).

It is easy to romanticize these centuries of hidden existence, imagining secret gatherings by moonlight and whispered prayers in mountain caves. Yet, the reality was often one of hardship, fear, and loss. Families could be scattered in an instant by raids or forced conversions. Leaders risked their lives to travel between far-flung communities. The fear of betrayal and exposure was ever-present. But through it all, the Ismailis held fast to a quiet confidence that they were guardians of a precious flame, a lineage that stretched back to Ali and the Prophet Muhammad himself.

In the 19th century, a significant turning point arrived. The 46th Imam, Hasan Ali Shah, better known as Aga Khan I, played a pivotal role in transitioning the community into a new era. Fleeing political turmoil in Persia, he settled in India, where he received the honorary title "Aga

Khan" from the Qajar dynasty. This move laid the groundwork for a more visible and organized Ismaili presence, especially in South Asia. Over time, the Aga Khan became not only a spiritual leader but also a central figure in guiding the community's social and economic development.

By establishing a strong base in India and eventually expanding his influence globally, the Aga Khan enabled the Ismailis to shift from scattered, secretive communities to a more cohesive, confident, and outward-facing network. This transformation marked the beginning of the modern Ismaili identity — one that embraces public service, education, and global engagement while staying deeply rooted in spiritual teachings.

As we look back at this long chapter of hidden survival, we see not just a story of suffering but a saga of incredible resilience and adaptability. The Ismailis proved that faith could survive — and even thrive — without grand monuments or public displays. Their strength lay in the hearts and minds of their people, in whispered prayers and secret gatherings, in the quiet conviction that the light must go on.

In the chapters to come, we will explore how this scattered but strong community blossomed under the leadership of the Aga Khans into a global network devoted to humanitarianism, education, and cultural preservation. The story of the Ismailis after Alamut is not just about survival — it is about transformation, reinvention, and the enduring power of a faith that refuses to be extinguished.

Chapter 6: The Aga Khan Legacy — A Modern Imamate

As the 19th century dawned, the world was changing at a dizzying pace. Empires rose and fell, colonial powers carved up vast swathes of the globe, and technology began to shrink distances once thought unbridgeable. Amid this whirlwind, the Ismaili community, which had endured centuries of secrecy and fragmentation, was about to step confidently into the modern world under a revitalized leadership: the Aga Khans.

The transformation began with Hasan Ali Shah, better known as Aga Khan I, the 46th Imam of the Nizari Ismailis. Born in 1804 in Persia (modern-day Iran), Hasan Ali Shah found himself at the center of political turbulence. Recognized by the Qajar Shah of Persia with the title "Aga Khan" in 1818, he initially held considerable influence. However, political disputes and conflicts with local rulers forced him into exile. In 1840, he fled to India, eventually settling in Bombay (now Mumbai).

For the scattered Ismaili community, Aga Khan I's move to India was momentous. It marked the beginning of a new chapter — one where the Imamate transitioned from a hidden, defensive posture to an open, visible leadership. In India, Aga Khan I established a strong base, forging relationships with British colonial authorities and local leaders. His charisma and diplomatic skills helped consolidate the various Ismaili groups under a unified banner, giving them a renewed sense of identity and belonging.

The groundwork laid by Aga Khan I set the stage for his successors. Aga Khan II, though his leadership was brief (from 1881 to 1885), continued efforts to modernize and unify the community. But it was his son, Aga Khan III, who would become one of the most influential figures in modern Muslim and global history.

Aga Khan III, born Sultan Mahomed Shah in 1877, became Imam at the young age of eight. Despite his youth, he possessed a visionary spirit and a remarkable intellect. Throughout his life, he wore many hats: religious leader, social reformer, diplomat, and statesman. His leadership spanned an extraordinary 72 years, during which he steered the Ismaili community into a new era of empowerment and global engagement.

Under Aga Khan III, the community began to emphasize education as a cornerstone of faith and progress. He famously declared, "If you have two children, educate both; if you can educate only one, educate the daughter first." This progressive stance on gender equality in education was revolutionary at a time when many societies around the world still denied basic educational rights to women.

He established numerous schools across South Asia and East Africa, focusing not just on religious instruction but on secular subjects as well — mathematics, science, literature, and languages. He believed that knowledge was a divine gift and that educating the mind was as vital as nurturing the soul. These schools became incubators for future leaders, entrepreneurs, and scholars, setting the foundation for an empowered and self-sufficient community.

Aga Khan III also played a significant role on the international stage. He was one of the founding figures of the All-India Muslim League and served as its president. Later, he represented India at the League of Nations, where he became the first Muslim president of the League's Assembly in 1937. Through these roles, he advocated for the rights of Muslims globally, promoting a vision of inclusivity, dialogue, and cooperation.

Perhaps one of the most remarkable aspects of Aga Khan III's leadership was his focus on community organization and welfare. He introduced systems of communal self-governance, establishing councils and welfare boards to manage local community affairs. These structures encouraged collective responsibility and participation, allowing the Ismaili community to address social, economic, and health issues more effectively. It was an early model of what we might today call "civil society," but deeply infused with spiritual values.

Upon Aga Khan III's passing in 1957, leadership passed not to his son or brother, as might have been expected, but to his grandson, Prince Karim Aga Khan IV. This choice, detailed in his will, surprised many but reflected his belief that the community needed a modern, forward-looking leader who could connect with a rapidly changing world.

Aga Khan IV was only 20 years old when he became Imam. Imagine the weight on his young shoulders: to guide a global community spread across continents, to uphold centuries of tradition, and to chart a course into the unknown future. Yet, from the very beginning, he approached his role with both humility and a bold vision.

Under Aga Khan IV, the Ismaili community blossomed into a truly global network. His leadership emphasized not just survival or self-preservation but active, positive contribution to society at large. He encouraged Ismailis to become fully engaged citizens of their respective countries, to integrate without losing their distinct spiritual identity.

Aga Khan IV founded the Aga Khan Development Network (AKDN), one of the world's largest private development organizations. Through AKDN, the community addressed healthcare, education, cultural preservation, rural development, and environmental sustainability. In East Africa, AKDN hospitals and schools became lifelines for entire communities, regardless of religious or ethnic background. In Central and South Asia, AKDN initiatives transformed isolated mountain villages into hubs of innovation and opportunity.

Beyond development projects, Aga Khan IV also championed the cause of pluralism and interfaith dialogue. He established institutions like the Global Centre for Pluralism in Ottawa, Canada, which fosters understanding and respect among diverse communities worldwide. His vision was clear: diversity is not a threat but a blessing, a source of strength and enrichment for humanity.

Under his guidance, Ismaili centers — beautiful architectural landmarks — sprang up in cities like London, Lisbon, Toronto, and Dubai. These centers serve as places of prayer but also as spaces for learning, cultural exchange, and community service. They embody the ethos of openness and hospitality that Aga Khan IV cherished.

By the early 21st century, the Ismaili community, once hidden in mountain fortresses and practicing in secrecy, had become a beacon of humanitarianism and progressive thought. Its members excelled in diverse fields: medicine, law, science, business, and the arts. Yet, throughout this remarkable transformation, they remained anchored in their faith, guided by the living Imam.

In 2025, after more than six decades of extraordinary leadership, Aga Khan IV passed away, leaving behind an indelible legacy. His son, Prince Rahim Aga Khan V, assumed the Imamate as the 50th Imam. Prince Rahim continues the mission with a focus on environmental stewardship and addressing the needs of the world's most vulnerable populations. His leadership promises to build on the firm foundation laid by his father and ancestors, guiding the community into an era that increasingly demands global cooperation and compassion.

The story of the Aga Khan legacy is not just a tale of religious leadership but a profound narrative of transformation — from secrecy to openness, from survival to flourishing, from local struggles to global impact. It is a story that resonates deeply in today's interconnected world, offering lessons on resilience, service, and the balance between tradition and innovation.

As we continue our journey, we will explore the spiritual heart of Ismaili belief — the theology that has inspired this remarkable history of adaptation and contribution. From the concepts of divine unity and the role of the Imam to the profound embrace of reason and inner truth, we will see how faith has been both the anchor and the compass for the Ismaili community.

Chapter 7: The Heart of Belief — God, Prophets, and the Living Imam

At the core of every faith lies a set of beliefs that guide, inspire, and sustain its followers through the ups and downs of life. For the Ismailis, their heart of belief is a dynamic tapestry woven from devotion to God, reverence for the Prophets, and a deep, living connection to the Imam of the Time. Together, these elements form not just a creed but a way of life — a spiritual compass pointing toward both divine love and service to humanity.

The foundation of Ismaili belief, like that of all Muslims, begins with the absolute oneness of God — *tawhid*. God is beyond all comprehension, all form, and all limitation. This belief in God's transcendence is not a distant, cold abstraction but a living reality that animates every breath, every act of kindness, every moment of reflection. The idea that God is both beyond and within creation weaves a profound sense of unity into the daily life of an Ismaili, inspiring them to seek the divine not only in prayers but in acts of service, compassion, and learning.

This belief in oneness naturally extends to the reverence for God's messengers, especially Prophet Muhammad, the "Seal of the Prophets." The Prophet is cherished not merely as a historical figure but as the ultimate conveyor of God's message to humanity — the Quran. His example, or *sunnah*, provides a moral and ethical framework that shapes every aspect of a believer's life, from personal conduct to social responsibility.

Yet, Ismailis also hold a unique and deeply cherished understanding of spiritual guidance after the Prophet's passing. While many Muslim traditions view religious leadership as a communal or scholarly enterprise, the Ismailis believe that divine guidance continues through a living line of Imams, starting with Ali ibn Abi Talib — the Prophet's cousin and son-in-law. Ali is considered not only a just and courageous leader but also the *wasiyy* (executor of the Prophet's spiritual heritage) and the first Imam.

This concept of the Imam as a living guide is central to Ismaili spirituality. For Ismailis, the Imam is not merely a symbolic figurehead or a distant historical ideal. He is a living, present, and divinely inspired leader who embodies the spiritual light (*nur*) that has been passed down through the ages. The Imam's role is to interpret the faith in the context of changing times, to guide the community toward spiritual and ethical growth, and to serve as a bridge between the finite human world and the infinite divine.

Imagine this relationship not as that of ruler and subject but more like that of a gardener tending a garden. The Imam nurtures, prunes, and guides each soul toward its fullest potential, helping it blossom in its unique way. Through this intimate, ongoing connection, every Ismaili feels directly linked to the divine message — not as a distant echo from the past but as a living melody harmonizing with the present.

This belief transforms the very understanding of religious authority. While other Muslim communities might look primarily to texts, jurists, or scholarly councils for guidance, Ismailis look to the Imam as the ultimate interpreter (*ta'wil*). His guidance evolves, taking into account new knowledge, social changes, and the diverse contexts in which the global community lives. This dynamic process of interpretation allows Ismailism to remain not just relevant but vibrant, meeting the spiritual and ethical needs of each generation.

Another profound aspect of the Ismaili understanding of the Imam is his role as the *hujjat* — the "proof" of God on earth. In a world often clouded by complexity and moral ambiguity, the Imam stands as a living sign of divine mercy and wisdom. This belief is not intended to create blind obedience but rather to inspire each individual to reflect deeply, to question sincerely, and to live responsibly.

The spiritual bond between the Imam and the community is further strengthened through *bay'ah* — the oath of allegiance. This is not a mere ritual formality but a personal, heartfelt commitment to follow the Imam's guidance in faith and in action. It symbolizes a sacred covenant of trust and love, reflecting the believer's dedication to both spiritual growth and ethical conduct.

Integral to this framework is the concept of *nur* — the spiritual light believed to be inherited by each Imam. This light is seen as a continuous thread linking back to the divine origin, illuminating the path for those who seek it. The *nur* represents wisdom, compassion, and the capacity to interpret God's will in the ever-changing circumstances of human life. It is this light that empowers the Imam to guide the community not only in matters of worship but also in social, economic, and intellectual endeavors.

This theological vision has practical, everyday implications for Ismailis. It inspires them to view their lives as an integrated whole, where spiritual and worldly responsibilities are not separate spheres but intertwined aspects of their faith journey. The pursuit of knowledge, engagement in society, caring for the environment, and promoting social justice are all expressions of worship, as much as prayers and meditations.

Furthermore, this belief fosters a profound sense of collective identity and mutual responsibility. The Imam's guidance encourages Ismailis to support one another, to engage in voluntary service (*seva*), and to extend compassion beyond their community to all humanity. It is a faith that is deeply inward and yet expansively outward — an invitation to grow personally while also contributing to the common good.

Historically, this living guidance has been a source of resilience and adaptability. During times of persecution, the Imam's guidance helped the community navigate dangers through *taqiyya* and hidden networks. In times of prosperity, it inspired them to build universities, hospitals, and centers of art and culture. Today, in a globalized world filled with both extraordinary opportunities and unprecedented challenges, the Imam continues to guide Ismailis toward living as conscientious global citizens.

The belief in a living Imam also shapes the Ismaili approach to religious pluralism. Recognizing the Imam as a living interpreter of the divine message encourages an openness to dialogue and cooperation with other faiths and cultures. It supports the idea that truth can be approached from multiple paths and that understanding others is a divine imperative. This has led Ismailis to actively promote interfaith initiatives, social inclusion, and the celebration of diversity.

The current Imam, Prince Rahim Aga Khan V, embodies this ethos as he leads the community into the 21st century. His focus on environmental sustainability, poverty alleviation, and cultural preservation reflects the same spiritual commitment to improving the quality of human life. It is an extension of the timeless mandate to serve creation as a form of service to the Creator.

As we reflect on this deeply interconnected belief system — God's oneness, the Prophet's finality, and the enduring, living guidance of the Imam — we begin to see why the Ismaili faith has been able to sustain itself for over a millennium through exile, persecution, and constant change. It is not just a set of doctrines but a living, breathing tradition that invites each person into an intimate relationship with the divine, mediated through the gentle, wise presence of the Imam.

In the chapters to come, we will explore how these theological principles find expression in the community's daily practices and rituals, in their emphasis on intellectual inquiry, and in their compassionate engagement with the wider world. The heart of belief is not a static monument but a flowing river — always moving, always nourishing, always inviting us to dive deeper.

Chapter 8: Unveiling Inner Truths — Esoteric Wisdom and *Ta'wil*

Imagine sitting in a small, candlelit room. The air is filled with the scent of ink and parchment, the gentle flicker of flames casting moving shadows on the walls. In a corner, a teacher speaks softly, guiding a handful of eager listeners through verses of the Quran. But these are no ordinary lessons — each word, each phrase is a doorway, opening into hidden worlds of meaning. This is the world of *ta'wil*, the esoteric interpretation of scripture, a practice that lies at the very heart of Ismaili spirituality.

To the Ismailis, the Quran is a living text — multilayered, dynamic, and rich with hidden wisdom. It is understood not only through its outward, literal meaning (*zahir*) but also through its inner, spiritual essence (*batin*). This distinction reflects a deep philosophical conviction: that reality itself is composed of both seen and unseen dimensions. Just as a seed contains the hidden potential of a tree, the outward words of scripture conceal an inner truth waiting to be unveiled.

Ta'wil — meaning "to return to the origin" or "to bring back to the source" — is the process of uncovering these deeper meanings. This is not simply a matter of creative interpretation but a disciplined, guided journey, often led by the Imam or learned scholars appointed by him. It requires not only intellectual effort but spiritual refinement, humility, and readiness to look beyond surface appearances.

Historically, *ta'wil* has been a powerful tool for Ismailis to adapt and thrive. In times when the community faced persecution, the emphasis on inward, personal understanding allowed the faith to survive in secret. Believers could outwardly conform to dominant religious practices while internally nurturing the true spirit of their tradition. It turned faith into a deeply personal sanctuary, an unassailable inner fortress.

But *ta'wil* is not merely a survival strategy; it is an invitation to transform one's whole approach to life. It teaches that every phenomenon — whether a religious ritual, a verse of scripture, or even a natural event —

has layers of significance. This spiritual lens encourages believers to seek meaning in everything, fostering a profound sense of wonder and interconnectedness.

Take, for example, the concept of fasting. In its literal form (*zahir*), fasting involves abstaining from food and drink during daylight hours, as practiced in Ramadan by many Muslims. But in Ismaili *ta'wil*, fasting also symbolizes abstaining from base desires and distractions, purifying one's thoughts, and focusing inward to receive divine light. Thus, physical discipline becomes a metaphor for spiritual self-mastery.

Similarly, the pilgrimage (*hajj*) in its exoteric form is a journey to Mecca, circling the Kaaba in ritual devotion. In the Ismaili esoteric tradition, this is complemented by the understanding that the true pilgrimage is the journey toward the divine within oneself, guided by the living Imam. Visiting the Imam is seen as the ultimate *hajj*, representing the spiritual homecoming of the soul.

This inward focus fosters a rich spiritual interiority. Ismailis are taught to view their religious life not as a set of rigid rules but as a journey of self-discovery, guided by compassion and intellect. The Imam plays a crucial role here, as the one who holds the key to the deepest levels of meaning. Without his guidance, the hidden layers remain locked, like a treasure chest without its key.

This approach also reflects the community's historical embrace of knowledge and intellectual inquiry. During the Fatimid Caliphate, for instance, the House of Knowledge (*Dar al-'Ilm*) in Cairo was a place where scholars engaged not only in religious studies but also in science, philosophy, medicine, and mathematics. The integration of spiritual and rational pursuits was a natural expression of *ta'wil* — a recognition that truth could be approached through multiple paths, all ultimately leading back to the divine source.

In the modern era, this tradition continues to shape Ismaili thought and practice. The emphasis on interpreting the faith to meet contemporary challenges has enabled the community to navigate the complexities of globalization, technological change, and cultural diversity. Rather than clinging to static forms, Ismailis are encouraged to engage actively with the world, to seek knowledge in all fields, and to view service to humanity as a form of spiritual expression.

Ta'wil also nurtures a culture of humility and openness. Recognizing that each verse, each symbol, has countless layers reminds believers that no single interpretation can claim total finality. This openness to multiple meanings supports a pluralistic outlook — a willingness to respect and learn from other faith traditions and perspectives. It is no surprise that Ismaili leaders have consistently championed interfaith dialogue and social harmony; these commitments are deeply rooted in their spiritual practice.

Furthermore, *ta'wil* encourages Ismailis to constantly renew their understanding of faith. This dynamic process means that religious practice is never stagnant. Instead, it evolves alongside the believer's growth and the changing context of the world. It allows the community to remain both rooted in tradition and responsive to new realities — a rare and precious balance.

In daily life, this esoteric approach manifests in subtle but powerful ways. It inspires Ismailis to reflect on their intentions behind every action, to cultivate inner purity alongside outer discipline, and to see challenges as opportunities for deeper insight. Even ordinary tasks, when approached with mindfulness and a quest for meaning, become pathways to spiritual growth.

Imagine an Ismaili artisan carefully weaving a rug. While his hands move over the threads, his mind contemplates the intricate patterns of existence, the interconnectedness of all things, and the hidden divine presence in the beauty he creates. Or consider a young student studying science; her exploration of the physical universe is not a distraction from faith but an act of devotion, an inquiry into the marvelous design of creation.

In this way, *ta'wil* transforms life itself into a spiritual text to be read, interpreted, and cherished. It teaches that every moment holds the potential for revelation, every encounter a lesson, every hardship a veiled blessing.

This profound relationship between the exoteric and esoteric is perhaps one of the most distinctive and beautiful aspects of Ismaili Islam. It weaves a golden thread through centuries of history, binding together diverse cultures and generations in a shared pursuit of inner light. It has enabled the community to endure persecution without bitterness, to embrace knowledge without fear, and to serve humanity without losing their spiritual compass.

As we move forward in this story, we will see how these theological principles give shape to daily practices and communal life — from unique interpretations of ritual to an enduring commitment to service and pluralism. The journey of *ta'wil* invites us all to look beyond the surface, to seek the divine whisper beneath the noise of the world, and to remember that every soul carries a hidden treasure waiting to be discovered.

Chapter 9: Mind and Spirit — The Embrace of Reason

Walk into an Ismaili center anywhere in the world — perhaps in Nairobi, Lisbon, or Toronto — and you will sense it almost immediately: a quiet reverence not only for prayer and ritual but also for books, learning, and thoughtful conversation. In classrooms and lecture halls, in science labs and art studios, you find Ismailis engaged in the search for knowledge with a zeal that is, in itself, an act of devotion. This love of learning, this harmony of mind and spirit, has been a cornerstone of Ismaili identity for over a millennium.

But why has reason been given such a prominent seat in Ismaili tradition? The answer lies deep in their theological foundations and historical experience. For Ismailis, faith is not meant to be a blind submission; it is a living, breathing journey that requires the full engagement of the intellect. They believe that God bestowed upon humans not only revelation through prophets but also the gift of *aql* — reason, intellect — as a divine tool to explore, understand, and act in the world.

The importance of intellect can be traced back to Imam Ali ibn Abi Talib, the first Imam, whose sermons and writings, collected in the *Nahj al-Balagha*, emphasize the role of the mind as a means to approach God. Ali taught that reason is a light in the darkness, a guide on the path toward understanding the divine mysteries. Later Imams, like Ja'far al-Sadiq, expanded on this, encouraging exploration of the natural world and philosophical inquiry as forms of worship.

Under the Fatimid Caliphate, this embrace of reason blossomed into a cultural golden age. In Cairo's Dar al-'Ilm — the House of Knowledge — scholars gathered to discuss everything from metaphysics to medicine, astronomy to poetry. They saw no contradiction between revelation and reason; rather, they believed that both emerged from the same divine source and complemented each other beautifully.

This integrative approach stood in stark contrast to rigid dogmatism. It allowed for an openness to new ideas and innovations, fostering a society where Christian, Jewish, and Muslim scholars could share knowledge, challenge each other's ideas, and collaborate. This intellectual atmosphere produced advances in medicine, architecture, mathematics, and the arts that rippled across the medieval world.

Ismailis inherited this ethos, carrying it through centuries of migration and hardship. Even when they were forced into secrecy and survival mode, they maintained a quiet but steadfast commitment to learning. Manuscripts were hidden, oral teachings carefully transmitted, and young minds nurtured with stories that emphasized curiosity and ethical reflection.

The emphasis on intellect also explains the modern community's deep commitment to education. In places like East Africa, where many Ismailis settled in the 19th and 20th centuries, they quickly established schools and scholarships, understanding that knowledge was the key to empowerment and self-sufficiency. In Central and South Asia, community schools became beacons of hope, especially for girls, embodying the community's progressive vision long before it became a global norm.

When Aga Khan III assumed leadership in the late 19th century, he built on this tradition by encouraging universal education for both boys and girls, founding hundreds of schools, and supporting higher education institutions. His forward-looking policies anticipated the global educational movements of the 20th century and helped transform Ismaili communities into hubs of intellectual vibrancy.

Aga Khan IV carried this vision further, establishing the Aga Khan University in Karachi in 1983 — the first private university in Pakistan. This institution is not only a center of medical and scientific excellence but also a symbol of the community's belief that education is a sacred trust. Similar initiatives, like the University of Central Asia and numerous educational programs under the Aga Khan Development Network (AKDN), reflect this same conviction.

But this love of reason is not limited to academic or scientific pursuits. It also shapes the way Ismailis think about faith itself. They are encouraged to ask questions, to explore spiritual concepts with critical thinking, and to engage with contemporary ethical dilemmas using both religious principles and rational thought. This dynamic interaction between faith and intellect allows the tradition to remain vibrant and responsive to the complexities of modern life.

For example, in an age of rapid technological change and global crises, many religious communities face the challenge of adapting without losing their core identity. The Ismailis, guided by the principle that revelation and reason are complementary, have approached issues like environmental stewardship, economic inequality, and pluralism not as threats but as ethical opportunities. These challenges become avenues to express faith in action — to live as stewards of creation and servants of humanity.

In personal life, this perspective empowers Ismailis to approach decision-making with a balance of heart and mind. Whether choosing a career path, raising a family, or engaging in community service, they are taught to weigh options thoughtfully, to consider consequences, and to seek harmony between personal aspirations and the greater good. This blend of spirituality and rationality fosters individuals who are reflective, compassionate, and socially engaged.

It also underpins their commitment to pluralism. Recognizing that human reason is diverse and shaped by different experiences and cultures, Ismailis embrace dialogue and cooperation with other faiths and communities. Rather than seeing differences as threats, they view them as opportunities for mutual learning and enrichment. This open-mindedness is visible in the design of Ismaili centers, which often include spaces for interfaith dialogue, cultural exhibitions, and public lectures.

The Global Centre for Pluralism in Ottawa stands as a monumental expression of this ethos. Founded by Aga Khan IV in partnership with the Canadian government, the center promotes respect for diversity as a foundational value of human society. Its work, from research to educational programs, echoes the community's long-standing belief that embracing reason and diversity is essential to building peaceful, inclusive societies.

In arts and architecture, too, this philosophy shines. Ismaili architects and artists often merge traditional Islamic motifs with modern design, using geometry, light, and open space to create environments that invite contemplation and connection. This aesthetic celebrates both heritage and innovation, embodying the community's balance of continuity and progress.

At its heart, the Ismaili embrace of reason is not about diminishing faith but about deepening it. It teaches that God's creation is a vast, wondrous book, written not only in scripture but also in the stars, in the human heart, and in the patterns of nature. Exploring this book with curiosity and reverence is seen as a form of worship, an ongoing quest to draw closer to the divine.

This harmony between mind and spirit — between knowing and believing — is a defining strength of the Ismaili tradition. It explains how a community that once hid in mountain fortresses can now lead in universities, hospitals, and global humanitarian efforts. It illuminates why Ismailis can remain deeply rooted in their spiritual heritage while confidently engaging with modernity.

As we continue our journey through this remarkable story, we will see how these principles shape everyday practices, from ritual life to social responsibility. The dance between intellect and devotion is not just an abstract ideal but a lived reality, one that inspires each Ismaili to see the world as a sacred space of endless learning and boundless possibility.

Chapter 10: Rituals Reimagined — Practices and Pillars

When people think of religious practice, they often imagine strict rituals, fixed postures, and ancient words chanted in unison. But within Ismaili tradition, religious practice is not merely about repetition or external observance. It is a dynamic, living expression of faith, deeply infused with meaning and always connected to the inner journey of the soul. In this chapter, we explore how Ismailis interpret and live out the foundational pillars and practices of Islam — and how they have reimagined them to reflect their distinctive esoteric philosophy.

Like all Muslims, Ismailis affirm the five traditional pillars of Islam: *Shahada* (declaration of faith), *Salah* (prayer), *Zakat* (charity), *Sawm* (fasting), and *Hajj* (pilgrimage). But Ismailis also recognize two additional pillars: *Taharah* (purity) and *Jihad* (spiritual struggle), making a total of seven pillars in their doctrine. This expanded framework reflects the community's commitment to a comprehensive, spiritually holistic approach to worship.

Let's start with the *Shahada*, the declaration of faith: "There is no god but God, and Muhammad is His messenger." For Ismailis, this fundamental statement is further deepened by their belief in the Imam of the Time as the continuation of divine guidance. The *Shahada* is not merely a phrase recited; it is a continuous reaffirmation of their commitment to God and to following the Imam as the living embodiment of divine light.

When it comes to *Salah*, or ritual prayer, Ismailis practice a unique tradition. While Muslims typically pray five times daily, the Ismaili prayer practice is simplified and infused with meditative depth. Communal prayers are often held at *Jamatkhanas* — community gathering spaces that serve as spiritual and social hubs. In these prayers, emphasis is placed not on elaborate physical movements but on the inner connection with God and the Imam. The atmosphere in a *Jamatkhana* during prayer is serene, with recitations that encourage personal reflection and collective unity.

These prayer gatherings also symbolize the community's commitment to solidarity. They serve as moments where members come together, regardless of social or economic status, to share not only spiritual but also emotional and social support. After prayers, it's common to see people sharing meals, discussing family matters, or collaborating on community projects. In this way, the spiritual practice seamlessly extends into community building.

The pillar of *Zakat*, or charity, is another area where Ismailis emphasize both outward and inward dimensions. Like other Muslims, Ismailis are required to give a portion of their wealth to support those in need. However, Ismailis also practice a special form of tithe known as *Dasond*, a voluntary contribution of a percentage of one's income directly to the Imam of the Time. These funds are used for community development projects, humanitarian aid, educational programs, and health services, benefiting both Ismailis and wider society. Through this system, charity becomes not only an obligation but an act of gratitude and trust — a recognition that material wealth is a divine blessing meant to be shared.

Next is *Sawm*, or fasting. While the literal fast during Ramadan is widely practiced across the Muslim world, many Ismailis interpret fasting in a more spiritual, symbolic way. For them, the deeper essence of fasting is self-restraint, purification of thoughts, and control over base desires. Some groups also observe specific fasts, such as the *Shukravari Beej*, a monthly spiritual practice. This interpretive approach reflects their larger commitment to *batin* (inner meaning), encouraging believers to focus on ethical and spiritual purification in daily life rather than strictly on abstaining from food and drink.

The *Hajj*, or pilgrimage to Mecca, is traditionally a central pillar of Islam. Ismailis, however, view pilgrimage in an expanded, symbolic sense. Many believe that the ultimate pilgrimage is to the living Imam, the bearer of divine guidance. Meeting the Imam, even briefly, is seen as a profound spiritual journey, an encounter that embodies the soul's return to its spiritual origin. While some Ismailis still undertake the traditional Hajj to Mecca, the spiritual pilgrimage to the Imam is often regarded as the most significant.

Beyond these five pillars, Ismailis emphasize *Taharah*, or purity. This pillar goes far beyond physical cleanliness. It refers to the purity of the soul, the clarity of intentions, and the ethical integrity of one's actions. Maintaining *taharah* is a daily commitment — not only through acts of cleanliness but also through kindness, honesty, and sincerity in relationships and endeavors. This pillar serves as a reminder that spiritual elevation begins with cultivating purity in every aspect of life.

The final pillar, *Jihad*, is perhaps one of the most profound yet misunderstood concepts. In Ismaili thought, *Jihad* is primarily an inner struggle — the constant effort to overcome ego, selfishness, and moral weaknesses. This "greater jihad" is seen as the true battleground where a believer refines the soul and aligns it with divine will. It stands in contrast to the external, militant interpretations often sensationalized in popular media. For Ismailis, this inner struggle is a lifelong quest, essential to personal and communal growth.

Each of these pillars interweaves the physical with the spiritual, the individual with the communal, and the ritual with ethical living. This integrative approach reflects the Ismaili conviction that religion is not confined to isolated acts of worship but permeates every facet of life.

In addition to these formal practices, Ismailis emphasize a strong tradition of voluntary service, or *seva*. Whether through local community projects, disaster relief efforts, or global initiatives under the Aga Khan Development Network (AKDN), service is considered an essential expression of faith. Acts of service — from mentoring youth to planting trees or assisting refugees — are seen as offerings to God, moments where divine love flows through human hands.

The architecture and atmosphere of *Jamatkhanas* also embody these principles. Designed not just as places of worship but as centers of learning, culture, and social welfare, they symbolize the fusion of spirit and community. In cities around the world, these centers stand as welcoming spaces, often featuring libraries, classrooms, and spaces for cultural events and dialogues. Here, one can see children learning about ethics, elders sharing wisdom, and volunteers organizing charity drives — all under the same roof where prayers echo softly.

Through this unique blend of rituals and ethics, Ismailis have created a religious life that feels at once ancient and modern, intimate and expansive. Their practices are not rigid blueprints but living expressions that evolve with context, guided by the Imam's interpretation. This flexibility allows each generation to find renewed relevance and personal connection in their faith.

At the heart of these practices lies a profound understanding: that religion is not merely about individual salvation but about collective upliftment. It calls each believer to transform themselves and, in doing so, contribute to transforming the world around them. It is a call to be gardeners of the soul and architects of a just, compassionate society.

As we move forward, we will see how these deeply held practices prepare the community to thrive in diverse societies across the globe, from East Africa to North America. We will explore how Ismailis weave their faith into public life and how their understanding of pluralism and service becomes a bridge to wider humanity.

Chapter 11: A Global Tapestry — The Modern Ismaili Diaspora

When you think of the Ismaili community today, you might picture a smiling volunteer in Vancouver helping at a local food bank, a medical researcher in London developing new treatments, or a teacher in the mountains of northern Pakistan introducing young girls to the world of science. This kaleidoscope of faces, professions, and locations captures the essence of the modern Ismaili diaspora — a truly global community connected by shared faith, values, and an unwavering commitment to service.

The Ismailis are among the most widely dispersed Muslim communities in the world, numbering about 12 to 15 million people across more than 35 countries. This global spread did not happen overnight. Rather, it is the result of centuries of migrations driven by persecution, political upheaval, trade, and, more recently, opportunities for education and economic growth.

Following the collapse of the Fatimid Caliphate and the destruction of Alamut, Ismailis sought refuge in remote mountain valleys, deserts, and far-off lands. In Persia (modern-day Iran), they survived in rugged mountain villages, preserving their traditions quietly. In South Asia, particularly in Gujarat and Sindh, Ismailis established vibrant communities, blending local customs with their religious heritage and becoming known as the Khojas.

By the 19th and 20th centuries, a new wave of migration began, driven by economic prospects and colonial shifts. Many Ismailis moved to East Africa — to Kenya, Tanzania, and Uganda — where they became successful traders, artisans, and entrepreneurs. With their strong work ethic and community support systems, they quickly rose to become influential contributors to local economies and civil society. In these new homelands, they built schools, hospitals, and community centers, embodying their ethos of service and self-reliance.

However, the story of East African Ismailis took a dramatic turn in the early 1970s. In Uganda, under the dictatorship of Idi Amin, tens of thousands of Asians, including many Ismailis, were expelled in 1972. Families who had lived there for generations found themselves uprooted overnight, their businesses seized, and their futures uncertain. Faced with this immense hardship, the community once again demonstrated its legendary resilience. With the help of Aga Khan IV and the global Ismaili network, many resettled in Canada, the United Kingdom, and other parts of Europe and North America.

Canada, in particular, became a major new home for Ismailis. The Canadian government welcomed them, impressed by their emphasis on education, entrepreneurship, and civic contribution. Over the decades, Ismailis in Canada have flourished, establishing successful businesses, excelling in academia and medicine, and becoming active participants in political and civic life. The iconic Ismaili Centre in Burnaby, near Vancouver, and the Aga Khan Museum and Ismaili Centre in Toronto stand as symbols of the community's integration and contribution to Canadian society.

In the United Kingdom, Ismailis similarly became an example of successful integration. The London Ismaili Centre, opened in 1985, serves as a spiritual, cultural, and social hub, fostering dialogue and community engagement. In the United States, the community has established roots in cities such as Houston, Chicago, and Los Angeles, and more recently, the striking new Ismaili Center in Houston reflects their growing presence and visibility.

Meanwhile, in Central and South Asia, the community remains deeply rooted despite historical and political challenges. In Tajikistan's Gorno-Badakhshan region and parts of northern Pakistan, Ismailis have lived for centuries, often in isolated, mountainous areas. Here, they continue to sustain rich traditions of poetry, music, and local crafts. Aga Khan Development Network (AKDN) initiatives in these regions focus on improving education, healthcare, and infrastructure, empowering communities to thrive while preserving their cultural heritage.

This global presence has shaped the Ismaili identity into a vibrant tapestry woven from diverse languages, cultures, and traditions. You can find Ismailis who speak Persian, Gujarati, Swahili, Urdu, Arabic, English, and French — often multiple languages fluently. They may prepare dishes influenced by Indian, Central Asian, or African cuisines, celebrate festivals with regional colors, and dress in styles reflecting their local environments. Yet, no matter where they live, Ismailis remain united by shared spiritual practices, ethical commitments, and loyalty to the Imam.

One of the most remarkable aspects of this global dispersion is the way it has encouraged a balance between adaptation and preservation. Wherever they have settled, Ismailis have integrated into local societies, contributing to economic and social development while maintaining their religious and cultural identity. The concept of *dual belonging* — being fully present and engaged citizens of their countries while also deeply rooted in their faith — is a hallmark of Ismaili life today.

The leadership of Aga Khan IV played a critical role in shaping this modern identity. He encouraged Ismailis to embrace citizenship fully, urging them to become active participants in their societies and to see their civic duties as expressions of faith. He famously advised, "Be proud citizens of wherever you live," emphasizing that serving the nation is a form of serving humanity, which in turn is service to God.

This guidance has inspired countless Ismailis to enter public service, volunteerism, and leadership roles. In Canada, for example, Ismaili volunteers played a significant role during the country's 150th anniversary celebrations, contributing over a million hours of community service. In East Africa, Ismailis have built and supported hospitals and schools that serve people of all backgrounds. In South Asia, they work to promote education, health, and disaster relief in some of the most remote regions.

Ismaili centers around the world further reflect this spirit of openness and engagement. These centers are not only places of prayer but also hubs for cultural exchange, interfaith dialogue, and community service. Visitors from all faiths and walks of life are welcomed, and programs range from art exhibitions and music performances to lectures on global issues and humanitarian projects.

The global Ismaili community also maintains a strong network of institutions and social structures. Local councils, volunteer organizations, and youth programs foster a sense of belonging and collective responsibility. Young Ismailis participate in leadership training, ethics classes, and service projects, cultivating the next generation of engaged, thoughtful, and compassionate citizens.

Technology, too, has played a pivotal role in uniting this far-flung community. Online platforms, virtual Jamatkhanas, and global broadcasts of important addresses by the Imam help connect Ismailis from the mountains of Tajikistan to the skyscrapers of New York. During the COVID-19 pandemic, these technological connections became lifelines, allowing spiritual gatherings, educational activities, and community support to continue uninterrupted.

Despite differences in geography, language, and local customs, the Ismaili community remains deeply cohesive. This cohesion is not enforced through rigid uniformity but nurtured through shared values: the pursuit of knowledge, compassion for others, respect for diversity, and devotion to the Imam. It is a model of global unity that celebrates local color and individual expression rather than suppressing them.

The story of the modern Ismaili diaspora is thus a story of bridges — bridges across oceans and mountains, across cultures and generations, across faiths and worldviews. It is a testament to the power of faith not as a wall that divides but as a thread that weaves people together into a global tapestry of humanity.

As we continue our journey, we will explore how this global community channels its shared values into service to humanity through initiatives like the Aga Khan Development Network. We will see how faith translates into action on a scale that uplifts millions and offers a shining example of what it means to live for others while remaining true to oneself.

Chapter 12: Service Beyond Borders — The Aga Khan Development Network

When we think of religious expression, we might first imagine prayer, fasting, or pilgrimage. But for the Ismailis, one of the most profound acts of faith is service to humanity — a living embodiment of spiritual devotion. Nowhere is this commitment more beautifully realized than in the work of the Aga Khan Development Network (AKDN), an extraordinary global force dedicated to improving the quality of life, regardless of faith, ethnicity, or geography.

The AKDN is not just an organization; it is a vision in action. Inspired by the guidance of the Imam, it embodies the belief that material well-being and spiritual fulfillment are deeply interconnected. Established and guided by Aga Khan IV, and now continued under Prince Rahim Aga Khan V, the network stands as a testament to the idea that serving others is an act of worship and a sacred responsibility.

Operating in over 30 countries, the AKDN addresses a vast array of human needs: health care, education, cultural preservation, economic development, environmental sustainability, and humanitarian assistance. Its approach is holistic, recognizing that poverty and marginalization are not simply economic conditions but complex interplays of social, cultural, and environmental factors.

One of AKDN's most visible impacts is in healthcare. Through a network of more than 700 health facilities — from small clinics in remote mountain villages to major hospitals in bustling cities — the organization provides care to millions of people each year. The Aga Khan University Hospital in Karachi, Pakistan, for example, is a world-class medical center offering advanced treatments and training the next generation of healthcare professionals. In East Africa, the Aga Khan Hospitals in Nairobi, Dar es Salaam, and Mombasa have become critical lifelines for local communities.

The commitment to education is equally deep and far-reaching. The Aga Khan University (AKU), founded in 1983, set a new standard for medical and nursing education in Pakistan and East Africa. Today, AKU also offers programs in teacher education, journalism, and public policy, equipping students with the skills to lead and transform their societies. Meanwhile, the University of Central Asia (UCA), established through a partnership among the governments of Kazakhstan, Kyrgyzstan, Tajikistan, and the Ismaili Imamat, brings higher education to some of the most remote and underserved mountain regions. In these places, young people gain not only technical knowledge but also the confidence and capacity to uplift their communities.

AKDN's commitment to early childhood education and primary schooling is equally strong. The network supports nearly 200 schools, including the Aga Khan Academies — a series of residential schools that blend rigorous academics with ethical leadership training. These academies aim to develop global citizens who are deeply rooted in their local cultures yet prepared to engage with the world.

Economic development is another cornerstone of AKDN's work. Through the Aga Khan Fund for Economic Development (AKFED), the network invests in projects that stimulate local economies, create jobs, and support entrepreneurship. These include telecommunications in Afghanistan, tourism initiatives that promote cultural heritage in East Africa, and banking services that empower small businesses. These ventures are designed not merely for profit but for long-term social impact, fostering sustainable growth and self-reliance.

AKDN's work in environmental stewardship demonstrates its forward-thinking approach to global challenges. The network supports renewable energy projects, reforestation efforts, and sustainable agriculture initiatives that protect ecosystems while improving livelihoods. In fragile mountain environments, where climate change threatens traditional ways of life, AKDN's interventions help communities adapt, preserving both natural and cultural heritage.

Cultural preservation is another passion woven into AKDN's mission. The Aga Khan Trust for Culture (AKTC) works to restore historic cities, monuments, and public spaces, breathing new life into centuries-old heritage. The transformation of Cairo's Al-Azhar Park, once a neglected dumping ground, into a lush urban oasis is a shining example. Similar projects in Zanzibar, Kabul, and Delhi celebrate cultural diversity while providing vibrant community spaces.

Yet perhaps the most moving aspect of AKDN's work is its unwavering commitment to the principle of inclusivity. The network serves people regardless of faith or background, guided by an ethic of compassion and a belief in the inherent dignity of every human being. In regions torn apart by conflict and division, AKDN projects offer a quiet, persistent counter-narrative — one of unity, healing, and shared humanity.

During crises and disasters, AKDN mobilizes swiftly. Whether responding to earthquakes in Pakistan, floods in Mozambique, or refugee needs in Syria, the network provides immediate relief and long-term rebuilding assistance. Its integrated approach means that even emergency interventions lay the groundwork for sustainable recovery and resilience.

All this work is underpinned by a philosophy deeply rooted in Ismaili theology: the idea that faith and worldly responsibility are not separate but intertwined. The Imam's guidance encourages believers to see service not as charity in the conventional sense but as an ethical obligation and a spiritual path. This teaching transforms service from a transactional act to a transformative experience for both giver and receiver.

This commitment to service also resonates deeply within local Ismaili communities. Volunteers play a vital role in AKDN's initiatives, offering their time, skills, and resources to support programs worldwide. This tradition of volunteerism is nurtured from a young age, with youth encouraged to engage in community service as a natural extension of their faith. From organizing health camps to teaching literacy classes and planting trees, these acts of service weave the community together and reinforce their shared purpose.

The spirit of AKDN can also be seen in its architectural projects. The Aga Khan Award for Architecture, established in 1977, celebrates designs that not only achieve aesthetic excellence but also improve quality of life, respect cultural identity, and promote environmental sustainability. These projects, whether a bridge in rural Bangladesh or a community center in Burkina Faso, highlight architecture's potential as a tool for social good.

As the AKDN moves forward under the leadership of Prince Rahim Aga Khan V, it continues to innovate and expand. Recent initiatives emphasize climate change mitigation, digital literacy, and economic inclusion for marginalized groups. This adaptive, forward-looking vision ensures that the network remains responsive to evolving global needs while staying true to its ethical foundations.

The story of the Aga Khan Development Network is a remarkable illustration of what can happen when faith is expressed through action on a global scale. It challenges the notion that religion is only about private piety or ritual observance, showing instead that it can inspire sweeping movements for social justice, human dignity, and environmental stewardship.

As we look ahead, we see a community and a network deeply committed to healing and uplifting a fractured world. Through AKDN, the Ismaili community demonstrates that spiritual values can animate the most practical of endeavors, turning compassion into clinics, wisdom into schools, and devotion into thriving gardens in the heart of cities.

In the next chapter, we will explore how these values of service and inclusivity extend beyond formal organizations, manifesting in the daily lives of Ismailis as they engage with broader society through pluralism, interfaith dialogue, and a profound tradition of volunteerism.

Chapter 13: The Spirit of Pluralism — Dialogue and Volunteerism

Imagine stepping into an Ismaili Centre anywhere in the world: London, Toronto, Lisbon, Dubai. You are greeted by serene architecture that blends contemporary design with traditional Islamic motifs, wide open courtyards that invite conversation, and welcoming faces offering tea and warm smiles. As you walk through its halls, you hear echoes of poetry readings, interfaith discussions, lectures on science and ethics, and community service planning meetings. These centers are more than places of worship — they are living embodiments of a core Ismaili value: pluralism.

Pluralism, in the Ismaili context, is not just a polite tolerance of others; it is an active embrace of diversity as a divine blessing. This principle is deeply rooted in the community's spiritual philosophy. For centuries, Ismailis have believed that God's creation is marked by variety — different colors, cultures, languages, and ways of worship — and that appreciating this diversity is an act of faith.

Under the leadership of Aga Khan IV, this principle has been expressed boldly and publicly. He has often spoken of pluralism as essential for peaceful, sustainable societies. "Pluralism is no longer simply an asset or a prerequisite for progress and development," he said. "It is vital to our existence." These are not empty words; they guide real, tangible initiatives around the world.

One such initiative is the Global Centre for Pluralism in Ottawa, Canada, established by Aga Khan IV in partnership with the Canadian government. This center serves as a hub for research, education, and policy dialogue aimed at fostering respect for diversity. Its programs engage governments, civil society, and educators to encourage more inclusive practices, whether through curriculum development, leadership training, or community workshops. By highlighting successful pluralistic societies and addressing barriers to inclusion, the center stands as a powerful counterforce to rising intolerance and polarization worldwide.

But pluralism is not only promoted at institutional levels. It is woven into the daily lives of Ismailis around the world. In their neighborhoods, workplaces, and schools, they actively engage with people of different backgrounds, forming bridges rather than walls. Whether organizing local food drives open to all, joining city councils, or participating in interfaith festivals, Ismailis strive to be exemplars of inclusive citizenship.

A key expression of this commitment is the tradition of *volunteerism*, or *seva*. From a young age, Ismailis are encouraged to serve — not only within their own community but for the benefit of society at large. The ethos is clear: service is an act of devotion and a way to express gratitude for life's blessings. Volunteers are involved in countless activities, including disaster relief, refugee support, environmental conservation, and educational mentoring. In many cities, it is not uncommon to find Ismaili volunteers supporting marathons, neighborhood cleanups, or organizing blood drives.

This culture of service was especially visible during the COVID-19 pandemic. Across the globe, Ismaili volunteers mobilized to deliver food to the elderly, support vaccination drives, and provide mental health resources. Virtual Jamatkhanas and community check-ins helped ensure that no one felt isolated, illustrating how ancient values can meet modern challenges with compassion and ingenuity.

Volunteerism is not an occasional act for Ismailis; it is built into the very fabric of community life. Councils, youth and women's groups, and social welfare boards are all run primarily through volunteer efforts. These structures create spaces where individuals of all ages can contribute their talents — whether by organizing cultural festivals, teaching ethics classes to children, or supporting global humanitarian projects.

At the heart of these efforts lies a deeply held belief in the dignity of every human being. This conviction is echoed in the Quranic verse cherished by Ismailis: "And We have honored the children of Adam" (Quran 17:70). The respect for human dignity naturally leads to a commitment to equality, justice, and peaceful coexistence.

Pluralism also shapes the community's approach to interfaith dialogue. Rather than seeing religious differences as threats, Ismailis view them as opportunities for learning and enrichment. Their centers often host interfaith prayer services, lectures, and cultural events where people of all backgrounds come together. This openness is more than hospitality; it is an intentional practice of building understanding and reducing prejudice.

Consider the story of a young Ismaili woman in Houston who organized a community dinner inviting neighbors from churches, mosques, temples, and synagogues. The event began with a simple meal but turned into an evening of storytelling, shared experiences, and newfound friendships. Or imagine a group of Ismaili youth in Nairobi who work with Christian and Hindu peers to plant trees in public parks, blending environmental stewardship with bridge-building across faith lines.

These stories reflect a long historical tradition. During the Fatimid Caliphate, Jews, Christians, and Muslims worked together in academic and artistic pursuits. That spirit lives on today, reinforced by the Imam's constant encouragement to see diversity as strength.

Pluralism, for Ismailis, is not about diluting one's identity. Instead, it is about strengthening it through genuine engagement with others. By understanding and appreciating other perspectives, one becomes more deeply aware of one's own beliefs and values. It is a process of mutual enrichment that strengthens community bonds and promotes global harmony.

This practice of pluralism is also visible in the arts and architecture of the community. The design of Ismaili centers, for instance, draws from multiple cultural traditions — Persian gardens, Mughal domes, and contemporary Western forms — to create spaces that are both rooted and inclusive. These spaces often include public gardens and courtyards, inviting everyone to pause, reflect, and connect.

The community's musical traditions also reflect this openness. From devotional *ginans* in South Asia, which incorporate Hindu poetic forms, to folk songs in Central Asia echoing Persian and Turkic influences, Ismaili music exemplifies cultural fusion while conveying deep spiritual meaning. This blending is not accidental but intentional, reflecting a long history of living among and learning from diverse cultures.

As we move deeper into the 21st century, the values of pluralism and volunteerism are more essential than ever. In a world increasingly divided by ideology, politics, and fear, the Ismaili community's example serves as a quiet yet powerful reminder that unity in diversity is not only possible but necessary for our collective future.

In everyday life, this commitment to pluralism and service creates ripple effects far beyond the walls of Jamatkhanas or community centers. It shapes compassionate doctors who listen deeply to their patients, ethical entrepreneurs who prioritize social good, and youth who lead with empathy and courage. It inspires families to open their homes to refugees, to support neighbors in need, and to stand up against injustice.

The story of pluralism and volunteerism within the Ismaili community is, at its heart, a story of love — love for humanity, for the earth, and for the divine spark within every soul. It invites each of us to consider how we, too, might live more openly, serve more generously, and connect more deeply.

In the next chapter, we will explore how these values find artistic and architectural expression, and how Ismailis celebrate beauty not just as an aesthetic choice but as a reflection of divine harmony and cultural heritage.

Chapter 14: Beauty and Legacy — Art, Architecture, and Culture

Imagine standing in the tranquil courtyard of an Ismaili Centre. The air is scented with flowering plants, the sound of water trickling in a fountain creates a soothing rhythm, and light dances across delicately patterned screens. Here, architecture does more than provide shelter — it invites contemplation, evokes wonder, and connects the human spirit to the divine.

For the Ismaili community, beauty is not a luxury or an afterthought. It is a vital expression of faith, a way of honoring the divine through the creation of spaces and objects that uplift the soul. Art and architecture are deeply integrated into Ismaili tradition, reflecting a long-standing belief that beauty and spirituality are inextricably linked.

This love of beauty can be traced back to the Fatimid Caliphate. During this golden age, Cairo became a beacon of learning, culture, and art. Under Fatimid patronage, master artisans and architects created dazzling mosques, universities, gardens, and palaces. The Al-Azhar Mosque, established in 970 CE, remains a testament to the Fatimid commitment to integrating spirituality and aesthetics. Calligraphy, geometric patterns, and architectural innovations all reflected a worldview that celebrated the harmony of form and meaning.

When the Fatimid era ended, the impulse toward artistic expression did not vanish. Instead, it adapted and traveled with the Ismaili community as they dispersed across regions. In Persia, Ismailis carried forward traditions of miniature painting, poetry, and intricate textile weaving. In South Asia, the community's devotional *ginans* merged Islamic devotional poetry with Hindu and Sufi literary traditions, creating lyrical works that continue to be sung in Jamatkhanas to this day.

In the mountain valleys of Badakhshan, the musical heritage took on unique forms. Traditional Pamiri music, with its haunting melodies and poetic lyrics, celebrates themes of love, nature, and spiritual longing.

Instruments like the rubab (a type of lute) and dutar (a long-necked string instrument) accompany songs that often carry hidden, esoteric meanings — another expression of the community's deep connection to *ta'wil* (inner interpretation).

These cultural expressions are not merely nostalgic or decorative. They serve as vehicles for transmitting spiritual teachings, ethical values, and communal identity across generations. A mother might sing a *ginan* to her child at bedtime, embedding lessons of love and divine unity into their earliest memories. A craftsman might carve geometric patterns into wood or stone, each angle and curve a silent prayer woven into daily life.

Architecture, in particular, has become one of the most visible and profound ways the Ismaili community expresses its values. Under the leadership of Aga Khan IV, the community has invested in creating spaces that reflect openness, inclusivity, and harmony with the environment. The Ismaili Centres — built in cities like London, Lisbon, Dubai, Dushanbe, Toronto, and Houston — are stunning embodiments of this vision.

These centers are more than places of worship. They are cultural beacons that invite the wider public to engage in dialogue, reflection, and learning. Designed by renowned architects, each center draws on regional influences while embodying universal Islamic design principles: geometric patterns symbolizing infinity, open courtyards inviting community, and natural light that symbolizes divine presence.

For example, the Ismaili Centre in Lisbon features serene gardens inspired by traditional Persian and Andalusian designs, creating a space where visitors feel both grounded and uplifted. The Toronto center, with its luminous glass dome and reflecting pools, invites contemplation of transparency and inner light. In each design choice, there is a conscious effort to blend function with metaphor, creating environments that nurture both the mind and spirit.

Beyond religious spaces, the Aga Khan Trust for Culture (AKTC) plays a crucial role in preserving and revitalizing cultural heritage worldwide. The AKTC's Historic Cities Programme has restored countless historic sites, breathing new life into urban spaces while honoring their cultural significance. The transformation of Al-Azhar Park in Cairo from a neglected landfill into a lush, vibrant urban oasis stands as a symbol of renewal and the community's commitment to environmental stewardship.

Similarly, the restoration of the ancient citadel in Aleppo, Syria, and the Mughal gardens in Delhi, India, demonstrates a reverence for the past paired with a forward-looking vision for community revitalization. These projects are not merely about preserving bricks and stones but about reviving cultural memory, fostering community pride, and providing shared spaces where people can connect across generations and backgrounds.

Artistic expression extends to contemporary fields as well. Many Ismaili artists, designers, musicians, and filmmakers draw on their rich heritage to create works that resonate globally. Whether crafting intricate jewelry inspired by Central Asian patterns or producing films that explore themes of migration and identity, these artists carry forward the tradition of blending the aesthetic and the spiritual.

This celebration of beauty also finds expression in everyday life. During festivals and community gatherings, colorful fabrics, intricate henna designs, and shared meals become expressions of joy and gratitude. Weddings and naming ceremonies are infused with poetry, music, and dance, transforming life's milestones into communal celebrations of divine blessings.

Importantly, this devotion to art and architecture is not inward-looking. It embodies the Ismaili commitment to pluralism and public engagement. By creating spaces and artistic expressions that are open and inviting, the community fosters dialogue, builds bridges across cultures, and offers a tangible expression of their core value: that beauty and compassion can heal divisions and inspire collective upliftment.

When an Ismaili Centre opens its doors to a visiting school group, when a restored park welcomes families of all faiths, when a public exhibition features calligraphy and photographs exploring themes of unity — these are moments when art becomes a silent ambassador of the faith's deepest values.

This approach to art and architecture is a powerful counter-narrative in a world often divided by walls, literal and metaphorical. It shows us that beauty can be a form of diplomacy, a language that transcends barriers and invites mutual understanding. In a time when the world feels increasingly fragmented, the Ismaili celebration of beauty stands as a gentle yet firm assertion that shared spaces and shared experiences can bring us together.

As we near the conclusion of this journey, we see how the Ismaili community's commitment to beauty, knowledge, service, and pluralism weaves together into a radiant tapestry. It is a legacy that honors the past while shaping a future rooted in compassion and creativity.

In the final chapter, we will explore what this enduring journey means not only for the Ismailis but for humanity at large — and what lessons we might carry forward as we seek to build a more just, beautiful, and compassionate world.

Chapter 15: An Enduring Journey — Lessons for the Future

As we reach the end of this story — or rather, this chapter of a much longer story — we find ourselves looking out over a vast, evolving landscape. We see mountaintop fortresses, bustling city centers, moonlit poetry gatherings, and classrooms alive with questions and laughter. We see hands tending to the sick, rebuilding after disasters, and planting gardens in forgotten spaces. Above all, we see a community moving through centuries with grace, resilience, and an unwavering commitment to serving both God and humanity.

The story of the Ismailis is, in many ways, a story of light: sometimes hidden and flickering in the dark, sometimes radiant and visible to the world. It is a light that has guided them from the shadowed mountain fortresses of Alamut to the shining glass domes of Ismaili Centers in global capitals. It is a light that burns in acts of kindness, in songs sung softly to children, and in ideas shared across cultures and continents.

But this story is not just for Ismailis. It offers a mirror for all of us — an invitation to reflect on how we understand faith, community, and our shared human journey. What lessons can we draw from the Ismailis' thousand-year journey of survival, adaptation, and flourishing?

Perhaps the first lesson is the power of living faith. In a world where religion can sometimes become rigid or weaponized, the Ismaili example shows us that faith can be a living, breathing companion — evolving with the times, responding to new contexts, and guiding people toward service and compassion rather than division. Their tradition of a living Imam ensures that spiritual guidance is not frozen in time but continually reinterpreted, keeping faith both anchored and relevant.

A second lesson is the embrace of reason and knowledge. The Ismaili tradition teaches that the pursuit of knowledge is not separate from spiritual life but an essential part of it. This integration of mind and spirit invites us to explore the world, ask hard questions, and engage with science and philosophy without fear. It is a reminder that curiosity and critical thinking can deepen rather than diminish our spiritual lives.

The third lesson lies in resilience. Faced with relentless persecution, displacement, and political upheaval, the Ismailis responded not with bitterness or withdrawal but with renewed commitment to community, learning, and service. Their survival was not simply about hiding or fleeing; it was about continuously finding creative ways to sustain their identity and contribute to society. They teach us that true resilience is not just the ability to endure but the courage to transform hardship into an opportunity for renewal and growth.

Closely tied to resilience is the lesson of adaptability. Whether in the bustling ports of Zanzibar, the mountain villages of Badakhshan, or the cosmopolitan neighborhoods of London and Vancouver, Ismailis have shown an extraordinary ability to integrate into new societies while preserving their spiritual essence. This balance — of belonging and distinctiveness, tradition and innovation — offers a powerful model for communities navigating the complexities of globalization and multiculturalism today.

A fourth, and perhaps most inspiring, lesson is the ethic of service. For Ismailis, service is not just an occasional act of charity but a core expression of faith. Through institutions like the Aga Khan Development Network and countless local volunteer initiatives, they have demonstrated that caring for others is one of the highest forms of worship. In this vision, faith moves beyond personal salvation to become a force for healing and upliftment in the wider world.

This commitment to service is intertwined with a profound respect for pluralism. In a time when societies are increasingly polarized, the Ismaili example of engaging openly with different cultures and faiths shines like a lighthouse. They show us that diversity is not a problem to be solved but a gift to be celebrated — a source of strength and creativity that can unite rather than divide.

Their approach to art and beauty further enriches these lessons. By creating spaces that are open, inviting, and harmonious, the Ismailis remind us that beauty is not just decorative but transformative. It has the power to bring people together, inspire reflection, and express our deepest values without words. Whether through music, poetry, architecture, or gardens, the community offers a quiet but powerful testament to the idea that beauty and faith can — and should — go hand in hand.

Perhaps the most moving lesson of all is the one we feel rather than read: the importance of love. Love for God, love for the Imam, love for family and community, and love for all of humanity. It is this love that has carried the Ismailis through centuries of migration and change. It is this love that pulses through their acts of service, their commitment to learning, their beautiful spaces, and their open arms to strangers.

As we reflect on these lessons, we are invited to ask ourselves: How can we embody these values in our own lives? How can we make our faiths, beliefs, and values living forces that guide us toward greater kindness and understanding? How can we use our own talents — whether in teaching, healing, building, or creating — to serve others and contribute to a more compassionate world?

The story of the Ismailis also reminds us that identity is not a static inheritance but a living legacy, something to be continuously nurtured, re-examined, and shared. Whether we belong to ancient traditions or newly formed communities, we each hold a piece of humanity's collective tapestry. By weaving our thread with intention, humility, and openness, we strengthen the fabric of the whole.

As we conclude this book, it is clear that the Ismailis' journey is far from over. Guided now by Prince Rahim Aga Khan V, the community continues to evolve, carrying forward its timeless values into an increasingly complex and interconnected world. Their story stands as both inspiration and challenge: a call to build bridges rather than walls, to seek wisdom rather than certainty, to serve rather than dominate, and to love rather than fear.

In the end, "Guided by Light" is not just the story of one community. It is an invitation to all of us — to find the light within, to share it freely, and to walk together toward a future illuminated by knowledge, compassion, and beauty. As we move forward on our own paths, may we carry this light with us, becoming small but steady beacons in a world that is ever in need of hope and healing.

And so, the journey continues — not as a conclusion, but as an eternal unfolding. One light guiding another, one act of kindness inspiring the next, and one story reminding us all that, no matter where we come from, we share the same sky, the same longing for meaning, and the same capacity to build a world of peace, beauty, and love.

Timeline of Major Events in Ismaili History

7th century CE

- Death of Prophet Muhammad (632 CE).
- Ali ibn Abi Talib becomes first Imam in Shia belief.

8th century CE

- Imam Ja'far al-Sadiq designates his son Isma'il as successor.
- Early division between Ismailis and Twelver Shia.

9th century CE

- Period of concealment (*dawr al-satr*), hidden Imamate.
- Missionary network (*da'wa*) expands into Persia, Syria, and North Africa.

909 CE

- Establishment of the Fatimid Caliphate in Ifriqiya (North Africa).
- Imam al-Mahdi becomes first Fatimid Caliph.

969 CE

- Fatimids capture Egypt and found Cairo as the new capital.
- Establishment of Al-Azhar Mosque.

1090 CE

- Hasan-i Sabbah captures Alamut Castle in northern Iran, founding the Nizari Ismaili state.

1094 CE

- Schism within Ismailism after Imam al-Mustansir's death; split into Nizaris and Musta'lis.

1256 CE

- Fall of Alamut to Mongols; dispersal and concealment of Nizari Ismailis.

13th–18th centuries

- Survival through hidden communities in Persia, Syria, and Central Asia (e.g., Badakhshan).
- Nasir-i Khusraw's missionary work in Central Asia.

19th century

- Aga Khan I (Hasan Ali Shah) moves to India; recognized by British colonial authorities.
- Establishment of Khoja Ismaili communities in South Asia and East Africa.

1885 CE

- Aga Khan III becomes Imam at age 8.

1937 CE

- Aga Khan III elected President of the League of Nations Assembly.

1957 CE

- Aga Khan IV (Prince Karim Aga Khan) becomes Imam.

1972 CE

- Expulsion of Asians from Uganda; resettlement of many Ismailis in Europe and North America.

1983 CE

- Establishment of Aga Khan University in Karachi.

2006 CE

- Opening of the Global Centre for Pluralism in Ottawa.

2014–2025 CE

- Expansion of Ismaili Centers worldwide (Toronto, Dubai, Houston, Lisbon).
- Ongoing global development initiatives through AKDN.

2025 CE

- Passing of Aga Khan IV; Prince Rahim Aga Khan V becomes 50th Imam.

Bibliography

Primary Historical Sources

- Daftary, Farhad. *The Ismāʿīlīs: Their History and Doctrines.* Cambridge: Cambridge University Press, 1990.
- Daftary, Farhad. *A Short History of the Ismailis: Traditions of a Muslim Community.* Edinburgh: Edinburgh University Press, 1998.
- Daftary, Farhad. *The Assassin Legends: Myths of the Ismailis.* London: I.B. Tauris, 1994.
- Virani, Shafique N. *The Ismailis in the Middle Ages: A History of Survival, a Search for Salvation.* Oxford: Oxford University Press, 2007.

Fatimid and Alamut Period

- Halm, Heinz. *The Fatimids and Their Traditions of Learning.* London: I.B. Tauris, 1997.
- Hodgson, Marshall G. S. *The Order of Assassins: The Struggle of the Early Nizârî Ismâʿîlîs Against the Islamic World.* The Hague: Mouton & Co., 1955.
- Ivanow, Wladimir. *Alamut and Lamasar: The Ismaili Strongholds in Iran.* Tehran: Ismaili Society, 1960.

Modern Ismaili Community and the Aga Khans

- Nanji, Azim A., ed. *The Muslim Almanac: Reference Work on the History, Faith, Culture, and Peoples of Islam.* Detroit: Gale Research, 1996.
- Nanji, Azim A., and Farhad Daftary. *The Ismailis: An Illustrated History.* London: Azimuth Editions in association with The Institute of Ismaili Studies, 2008.
- Aga Khan Development Network. *Annual Reports and Program Summaries.* Various years.

Ismaili Thought and Theology

- Nasr, Seyyed Hossein. *Islamic Life and Thought*. Albany: State University of New York Press, 1981.
- Corbin, Henry. *History of Islamic Philosophy*. London: Kegan Paul International, 1993.
- Shafique N. Virani. *Islamic Thought in the Dialogue of Cultures*. Toronto: University of Toronto Press, 2016.

Pluralism, Service, and Cultural Heritage

- Global Centre for Pluralism. *Annual Reports*. Ottawa, various years.
- Aga Khan Trust for Culture. *Architecture in the Islamic World: Past and Future*. Geneva: The Aga Khan Award for Architecture, 1983.
- Karim H. Karim, ed. *Pluralism and Globalization in Ismaili Muslim Communities*. London: The Institute of Ismaili Studies, forthcoming.

Supplementary and General References

- Blank, Jonah. *Mullahs on the Mainframe: Islam and Modernity Among the Daudi Bohras*. Chicago: University of Chicago Press, 2001. (for comparative context).
- Lewis, Bernard. *The Assassins: A Radical Sect in Islam*. Oxford: Oxford University Press, 1967.
- Various articles and publications from *The Institute of Ismaili Studies* (London), including online resources and monographs.

Glossary

Aga Khan
Title given to the hereditary Imam of the Nizari Ismailis since the 19th century, starting with Hasan Ali Shah (Aga Khan I). The Aga Khan serves as both spiritual leader and guide for the community.

AKDN (Aga Khan Development Network)
A global network of institutions founded by the Aga Khan to improve quality of life through initiatives in health, education, culture, rural development, economic development, and the promotion of pluralism.

Alamut
A mountain fortress in northern Iran, captured in 1090 CE by Hasan-i Sabbah. It became the stronghold and intellectual center of the Nizari Ismailis during the medieval period.

Ali ibn Abi Talib
Cousin and son-in-law of Prophet Muhammad, considered by Shia Muslims, including Ismailis, as the first Imam and rightful successor to the Prophet.

Batin
The inner, esoteric meaning of religious texts and practices. Contrasted with *zahir*, or the outward, literal meaning.

Bay'ah
An oath of allegiance given by Ismailis to the Imam of the Time, signifying spiritual commitment and loyalty.

Da'wa
Missionary or summoning activity in Ismaili tradition; refers to the organized effort to spread the teachings of the Imams.

Dasond
A voluntary tithe given by Ismailis, typically a percentage of income,

contributed to support communal and humanitarian projects overseen by the Imam.

Dawr al-satr
"Period of concealment" during which the Ismaili Imams were hidden from public view for safety and survival.

Fatimid Caliphate
A Shia Ismaili caliphate that ruled parts of North Africa, Egypt, and the Middle East from 909 to 1171 CE, establishing Cairo as its capital.

Fidā'ī
A "devoted one"; historically, members of the Nizari Ismailis who carried out targeted missions (sometimes including assassinations) to protect the community during the Alamut period.

Ginans
Devotional hymns sung primarily by South Asian Ismailis (Khojas), blending Islamic spiritual themes with poetic traditions of the Indian subcontinent.

Hajj
Pilgrimage to Mecca, one of the five pillars of Islam. In Ismaili understanding, also symbolically refers to the spiritual journey toward the Imam.

Hujjat
A high-ranking spiritual representative in Ismaili daʻwa hierarchy; also means "proof" of God.

Imam
A spiritual leader and guide considered to be divinely appointed. In Ismaili theology, the Imam of the Time is seen as a living, present guide continuing the spiritual authority from Ali.

Jamatkhana
A congregation hall where Ismailis gather for communal prayers, ceremonies, and community events.

Jihad
In Ismaili interpretation, primarily refers to the inner spiritual struggle against ego and base desires; known as the "greater jihad."

Khojas
A group of South Asian Ismailis, historically converted from Hindu communities and known for their distinctive devotional traditions.

Nasir-i Khusraw
An 11th-century Persian poet, philosopher, and Ismaili missionary, influential in spreading Ismailism in Central Asia.

Nur
"Light"; symbolizes divine guidance passed through the lineage of Imams.

Shahada
Islamic declaration of faith: "There is no god but God, and Muhammad is His messenger." Ismailis include allegiance to the Imam as an extension of this commitment.

Sawm
Fasting; one of the five pillars of Islam. For Ismailis, also symbolizes spiritual purification and self-restraint beyond physical abstinence.

Shukravari Beej
A specific devotional observance or fast observed monthly by some Ismailis, particularly in South Asia.

Ta'wil
Esoteric or inner interpretation of religious texts, central to Ismaili spiritual practice.

Taqiyya
Practice of concealing one's faith to avoid persecution while maintaining inner belief.

Taharah
Purity; one of the seven pillars in Ismaili thought, encompassing both physical cleanliness and moral or spiritual purity.

Zakat
Almsgiving; one of the five pillars of Islam, requiring Muslims to give a portion of their wealth to those in need. Ismailis also give *Dasond* as an additional expression of generosity and devotion.

Zahir
Outward, literal meaning of religious texts and practices, contrasted with *batin*, the inner meaning.

www.ingramcontent.com/pod-product-compliance
Lightning Source LLC
Chambersburg PA
CBHW060418050426
42449CB00009B/2008